MW01487719

Excuses don't get results.
-Anonymous

----- Table of Contents -----

Prologue

PART I
Growing Pains

PART II
Taking Responsibility

Prologue

I haven't run in two years, possibly more. It's not something I'm proud of. In fact, I'm quite embarrassed about it. I had built a life out of running, and I let it go for such a long period of time that I've honestly forgotten exactly how long it's been.

Don't get me wrong; it's not like I was going to win a marathon or become the next great ultra-runner – that was never in the cards. However, considering where I came from and what I had to go through just to be able to walk, I shouldn't have let it go for so long.

Of course, I feel that I have my reasons and I would think that most would agree that requiring four different emergency surgeries on four different continents, discovering that I had a tumor or ripping my leg open down to the bone and from shin to knee are all solid reasons to take some time off.

And to be fair to myself, they were good reasons to take breaks. But to be honest with myself, they weren't good enough reasons to let running go for so long. Not in my opinion. They were simply excuses to let one of the most important aspects of my life get away. Or, if I was really being honest, maybe I used them as opportunities to avoid running rather than continuing on and risking possible failure.

You see, running has always been very difficult for me considering I was born with a birth defect. However, now that I'm a little older and a little wiser, I understand that my biggest issue was never how I was born, but rather my ability to fall victim to my own self-destructiveness. It's so much easier to not try than to risk failure. We can always explain why we didn't do something; we know the excuses and they flow easily enough. However, explaining failure seems more difficult.

So, to me, nothing that happened in the past handful of years amounted to a good enough reason to quit but did provide some great excuses. I know they're excuses because those unfortunate experiences pale in comparison to what I had to endure in my life before each of those things happened. After each setback I should have forced myself to get back to running as quickly as possible. I shouldn't have allowed the negative thoughts to dictate my actions so many times.

Besides, for me it wasn't just a sport that I was giving up on; it was my identity. I've built my entire life and livelihood around running, as difficult as it has been. For the past two decades I've taught thousands of people to run, both online and in person, I've run races all over the world and have operated my travel agency for runners since 2004. And that's all after being told that I would spend my life struggling to walk and that running would never be possible. So when I did run, I was beating my demons. But as it would turn out, I was only a few steps ahead of them. Perhaps I was using running as a way to keep them at bay but eventually they caught up to me. I gave in to those demons, the excuses. Rather than let those horrendous experiences only sideline me, I let them completely derail me.

I let go of everything for which I had worked so hard and so long. I slipped, then fell. I let my excuses get the better of me.

Since first struggling to walk at three and then having to relearn at eleven years of age, I had been climbing a mountain to get to where I was with my running. I suppose I hadn't realized how far up that mountain I had actually gotten until I started falling back down it. Although I haven't fallen all the way back to where I first started, to gain back even half that lost distance seems extremely daunting. I know some big odds are stacked against me. I also know that the odds of failure are high. Some may even write me off, if they haven't already.

But that's OK. I have no issue with what others think of me; it's what I think of me that I care about. Nothing else. And to say that I'm disappointed in myself is a huge understatement. However, it's also my biggest motivator.

I just need to realize that I simply lost my footing and now have some ground to make up. It doesn't matter whether that takes me a few years or the rest of my life. It just is what it is. It's the life I've created for myself and by very specific design. And I'm damn proud of that design! So, the decision is already made: I'm moving forward, not backward. It's nothing more than another challenge. My life has been full of challenges, but honestly, I'm extremely grateful for every one of them. They've pushed me to where I am today and will continue pushing me to where I need to be tomorrow.

This is the true story of a very unlikely person, definitely not born to run, who overcame a huge set of obstacles and a larger set of excuses to create a charmed life of traveling and running the world, against all odds.

PART I

Growing Pains

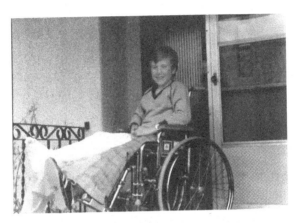

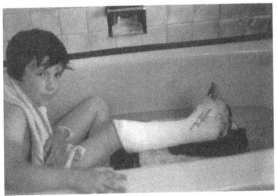

DUBAI, UNITED ARAB EMIRATES 2012

It's six in the morning and already closing in on 35 degrees Celsius. I look out my hotel window, rubbing my eyes and trying to see more clearly as everything seems blurry. I quickly realize that it's not my vision but the haze coming off the ground from the heat.

In the distance, the world's tallest building looms, beckoning me. It doesn't look that far away but here in the desert, everything seems closer than it is – especially when it's a building that towers an astonishing 163 stories.

Still, I think, I can run there and back. Right?

It's not a question I'm sure I can answer. However, regardless of where I make it to, I'm heading out into the heat to run. It's not my ideal run but I've already started putting on my running shorts. I've already made the decision and as much as I want to crawl back under the blankets in my air-conditioned room, I know that's not an option. I'm on autopilot and I know that if I even consider not running for a moment, I'll quickly find myself back in bed. I have no shortage of excuses, especially here in Dubai, where the weather, even at this early hour, is extreme.

I remember hearing John Stanton, the founder of the Running Room, give a speech about battling the desire to not run. He said, quite simply, even when you don't want to run, put on your running gear and see what happens. It's wonderful advice and it works well, so I follow his suggestion. I finish dressing while battling a mountain of good excuses to not run.

2

A few minutes later I'm downstairs in the lobby, where the temperature is a cool 21 degrees. A comfortable 21 degrees. An inviting 21 degrees. Beyond the two sets of front doors is another story altogether. I know this run will be a challenge but it's exactly this type of challenge that I live for, so I take a deep breath and start heading out.

I manage to make my way to that little space between the inside doors and the outside doors. It's that little buffer between the lobby and the outside world that, in Canada, we use to prevent the blast of cold winter air from directly entering the building when the outside doors are opened. Here in Dubai, it's used to keep out the blast of hot air. Even between these two sets of doors, where it's also air-conditioned, I notice a substantial difference in the temperature.

This heat is going to be overwhelming, I think. *I can always turn back, it's not too late.*

But I can't. I can't because if I back down now, what's to prevent me from backing down tomorrow? The day after?

I think about what life was like before running and how long it had taken me to get to where I'm at. I think about all the surgeries, the specialists who told me I could never run, the orthotics and chiropractors, the custom-made shoes, lifts, metal braces that lined my legs, wheelchairs, crutches and, of course, the pain. I also think about how much better my Crohn's is when I'm running. I realize there's no question that I'm heading out the next set of doors. I'm in Dubai and I'm going to log this run because this is what I do: I travel the world and run. Today, again, I'm going to win over my excuses. I'm going to beat my demons.

I take the deepest breath I can manage, then head out into the blistering heat.

3

Dubai gets ridiculously hot. Surface-of-the-sun hot, or so it seems. That's clearly an exaggeration, but temperatures can easily hit north of 50 degrees Celsius, and that's not exaggerating. I'm pretty sure today will be right up there.

I´ve made it only a few feet from the front doors and already I can feel the heat sucking away my energy. I look towards that monstrous building, the Burj Khalifa, way off in the distance and wonder if I can really make it. I purposely didn't check how far away it was, but now I regret that decision. Looks can be dangerously deceiving.

I turn off the brain and start running. That's another trick – not thinking. Just one foot in front of the other. Let the legs take over. Left, right, repeat.

I start with a slow jog, intending to pick up the pace after I reach the end of the hotel parking lot. It's not about warming up the muscles, as my legs already feel like they're on fire. It's about trying to save a little energy while not throwing up.

4

In the 1990's and before traveling like I do now, I really didn't care for the heat. I much preferred the cold. I remember the days of running in shorts and a t-shirt while the wind whipped and the temperature dropped to -15 degrees Celsius. Now it's quite the opposite; I feel very comfortable in 35-degree heat and I'm borderline miserable if it's less than 20 degrees above. I guess that's the product of spending most of my time in the tropics for the past 13 years.

Yet here in Dubai I am not comfortable at all as this is a whole new level of heat altogether. My mouth and throat are dry despite the fact that I'm constantly sucking up water from my bottle. And my water bottle, though it came out of the fridge just three minutes earlier, does nothing to cool me down, as the water is already hot. I start thinking about my lofty goal this morning, then question my sanity. I've gone for some crazy runs in my lifetime including some that have pushed the envelope way too far, but this definitely seems dangerous.

Rather than think about what's not right with this run, I try to focus on what *is* right. I'm in Dubai, for starters – a place I've always wanted to visit. The city is incredible and running through it will be a dream. I try to focus on the slight breeze, but it's not helping me cool off. It actually makes me feel like I'm standing too close to a campfire. I breathe deeply but the air burns all the way down and into my lungs. My attempts at being positive are failing terribly.

5

It's hard to believe but I've only run 200m or so. I now realize that reaching the Burj Khalifa is no longer an option. I want to turn around and head back, already beaten by the incredible heat. My water bottle, just a few minutes into my run, is already half empty and what's left feels close to boiling. I realized that I would literally die before I got to that building.

I remember running in the great Gobi Desert of China where it was also unbelievably hot but nothing like what I'm experiencing here. Still, I had gone blind in one eye for about 12 hours due to extreme dehydration and needed 6 bags of IV to bring me back to some resemblance of the living. They aren't pleasant memories, but they come rushing into my head for a reason. I realize I'd be a fool to attempt running to the Burj Khalifa, or, even a quarter of the way there.

6

I reach the end of the parking lot and instead of heading onto the main road and towards the city, turn and run along the side of the hotel hoping to make it at least once around the property.

I'm disappointed that I had to alter my run but at the same time I'm happy that I didn't give up while still in bed. My intentions were good; I didn't give into the excuses.

Instead of running to the world's tallest building I log the third shortest run of my life but definitely one of the hardest. I run just over one kilometer - a single loop around my hotel - before returning to my room utterly exhausted and with a decent dose of heatstroke.

As I stand in the shower, the cold water running over my burning skin, I smile to myself, grateful for the run and the challenge despite the outcome. Today has been a victory, albeit a small one, and I can only hope that tomorrow I'm just as strong.

I made it to the Burj Khalifa, but via taxi

Chapter 1 – Not Born to Run

In the summer of 1974, in a frantic delivery room in Richmond, British Columbia, Canada, my mother gave cesarean birth to a large, chubby and bald baby. I like to think I've changed a lot since then, but those things still mostly apply.

I ended up being a last-minute cesarean birth as my right foot was caught in my mother's ribs. She tells me that I kicked a lot during her pregnancy and that's probably how my foot ended up where it did. I, on the other hand, like to think that I started my life of running prenatal.

Regardless of how it happened, having my foot stuck some place it didn't belong for an extended period of time, and while my bones were growing, meant that I came out a little less than perfect.

I was born with a Clubfoot, meaning that my right foot was bent in half and my toes touched my heel. To complicate things further, my right leg was rotated outwards.

Typically, being born with a Clubfoot isn't that big of a deal. In fact, I've met a few different runners who were born with not just one Clubfoot, but two. Over-achievers in my opinion. I met them both during different marathons. I suppose they saw my leg and decided to chat with me. They both had assured me that their feet and legs looked and functioned the same as the average person's. However, they were very different from mine.

The difference between what happened to each of them at birth and what happened to me at birth was a few minutes of time spent by the delivering doctor. The attending doctor rectified their Clubfeet immediately upon delivery by bending their feet back into position, then applying casts. Standard procedure and simple, quick and painless (hopefully). Problem solved.

That wasn't my experience. Instead, there was some sort of breakdown in communication in my delivery room. Rather than having my problem resolved on the spot, I wasn't properly tended to for three days. When the hospital staff realized the mistake, the bones in my twisted foot and leg had set, thus sealing my fate.

Don't get me wrong. I'm not complaining. In fact, quite the opposite. I realized years ago that I should be – and am – very grateful for what happened. Being born with a birth defect has led me down an amazing path that I don't think I would have taken otherwise. Plus, it's made me realize that the only limits in life are those with which I choose to burden myself with. This has served me in many ways. My situation has been a driving force, giving me countless opportunities, and has pushed me to levels I may not have achieved otherwise. It's allowed me to help and inspire others, write articles and books, give lectures in Canada and overseas and even build a business and my entire life around two of the most important things to me: running and traveling. And all because of a deformed right foot and leg. It's given me purpose; the purpose to be more than anyone expected of me and more importantly, much more than I expected of myself. And all because someone forgot to bend my foot and leg a little.

I obviously don't know how my life would have turned out with two normal-looking and operating feet and legs, but I honestly couldn't have dreamed up a better life if I tried. That being the case, how could I ever be upset or angry? Instead, I'm beyond grateful for all it has brought me, including the challenges.

2

Of course, it's easy to look back now knowing how things would turn out. However, at the time and going through all the surgeries, I could not have guessed that I'd eventually be running marathons and beyond, especially because I was repeatedly told by doctors that I would always struggle just to walk and that running would never be possible.

In fact, if there were any constant reminders from my doctors, it was either about the things I would not be able to do later in life or about the things I would have to endure later in life. They told me that I would not be able to walk without special braces, shoe lifts and a cane all my life. Then they spoke about the chronic back pain I was going to have due to my poor body mechanics. Headaches, they said, would be common due to the chronic pain and I would always have a substantial limp.

That's a good-sized list of things to scare a young child, but more than anything, the idea of not ever being able to run or get involved in sports, bothered me more than the rest.

I also recall being confused by what they had to say. I just couldn't understand how they could tell me what I could or could not do in the future. And even if they honestly thought that way, why would they want to tell me? Perhaps they just wanted to be realistic and prevent me from getting my hopes up, but in the end, throwing around words like that only serves to limit people.

The truth is, everything is impossible until someone finds a way to do it. Then it is no longer impossible.

Of course, this is what I've grown to understand. I clearly didn't think like that when I was a kid going through the surgeries. Fortunately, however, what worked for me then was very simple: I rebelled and chose not to listen to their words and limitations. I was a child desperate to go outside and play, to get involved in sports and run. Or simply put: to be a kid. So every time they tried to set another limit for me, I simply pushed myself more. Starting early in my life I decided to look for possibility every time someone pointed out what was impossible.

3

Staying optimistic was important as it took me until I was 11 years old to get through all the surgeries, casts, shoe lifts, crutches and wheelchairs. At one point, I even had something similar to those Forrest Gump leg braces, except with a steel plate connecting both of my shoes so that I couldn't walk. I was literally propped up in a corner or sat on the floor, unable to move around. I spent a disproportionate amount of my youth in hospitals or just wheelchair bound. This was during a time when wheelchair ramps didn't exist, doorways weren't designed to accommodate a wheelchair's width and handicapped bathrooms hadn't been thought up yet. Or at least, none of that existed in the small Albertan town where I grew up. However, I always found a work-around for stairwells, high curbs and small bathroom stalls.

4

In total, I would have four major surgeries on my right leg and foot and double-digit casts, starting when I was just 72 hours old and finishing around the time of my 11th birthday.

The first three surgeries focused on different ways of forcing my foot open and reducing the extreme curve and ball-like shape of my foot.

During my first surgery, the surgeon opened the back of my ankle and did something to stretch out the tendons, allowing the foot to open more. It worked only a little and far from enough to rectify the issue. Discussions about my second surgery began while I was still in the recovery room.

During my second surgery, around the time of my second birthday, the surgeon opened the top and both sides of my right foot, then swapped the position of the tendons to permit the foot to open more. Again, this helped but my foot was still substantially twisted and curved. Having that second surgery at the age I did meant postponing my attempts to learn to walk. However, I suppose that didn't matter as walking around with one normal foot and a ball for the other foot wouldn't have done much for me.

That second surgery led to a third one which once again involved moving around more tendons. Like with the two previous surgeries, the surgeons were able to only partially correct the situation. Despite their best efforts, my right foot and leg would remain deformed.

I was eventually told that I had to accept the fact that there was nothing else they could do. This was bittersweet – bitter for obvious reasons and sweet because I could finally put the doctor visits and surgeries behind me and move on with my life.

5

The idea of moving on was important to me as it had been a game of back and forth for many years. Before each surgery, my mother and I would be promised that I would be able to do so much more once I got through and recovered from the next, upcoming surgery. Then after that surgery, I was told that they had been unable to completely rectify the issues, however, they could schedule me for another surgery during which they would try something else. The surgeons then proceeded to go through the list of things that I wouldn't be able to do; their list of limitations that I ended up ignoring.

The hospital visits, surgeries, casts, wheelchairs and crutches were becoming tiring and disappointing. Plus, I was starting to notice other ways in which the surgeries were affecting my life.

The biggest side effect was that I had put on a lot of weight from spending most of my childhood in a wheelchair or on crutches. When I wasn't in a cast and was able to hobble around a bit, I found it increasingly difficult to keep up with my friends due not only to my foot and leg issues but also to my newfound obesity.

It was disappointing as when I hadn't recently had surgery, I managed to keep up with friends a little more and participate in some casual sports (albeit with mediocre success at best). I was the kid chosen last when teams were picked at school, however, I always understood why and never held it against my friends. In any other situation my friends were always there to help by pushing my wheelchair, helping me carry my books and the like.

However, then came the additional weight and things went from bad to worse. I'm sure my friends didn't think any differently of me, but I did. My size constantly embarrassed me. As anyone knows who has battled obesity or even a few extra pounds, it's hard to quiet those damaging, negative voices in the head.

I forced myself to go out and join my friends despite being trapped in a body that wasn't mine and knowing that I would be chosen last. I did it because I also knew there would be months of time when I would be completely sidelined, wishing I could join them, a full leg cast sticking out in front of me as a constant reminder of what I couldn't do.

When I was finally told that the doctors had done all they could for me, I was happy knowing that there wouldn't be any more back and forth. I would recover from my third surgery, get on with my life and hopefully start losing weight.

6

I had finally recovered from my third major surgery, gotten through the physical therapy and adapted to getting around and I honestly thought I was finally finished with all the surgeries. Then, once again, came a new surgeon and a new promise.

I had already lived through a lot of broken promises about what could be done for my foot and leg. However, when your doctor introduces you to a new surgeon and to his ideas and the very likely possibility of a better life, it's hard to not listen.

The surgeon had been referred to me by my foot specialist and he felt that he could make a real difference in my life. He didn't claim that he could solve all my issues, but he did think he would be able to both rotate and flatten my right foot. This would align it better with my body, making walking a lot easier and perhaps preventing constant pain or discomfort.

That was good news, assuming it would work. What he wanted to do, however, made me very uncomfortable.

He explained that he wanted to break my ankle, remove a small cross-section of bone from my lower leg, rotate my foot to lessen its awkward angle and then piece me back together with a titanium rod running from just below my knee and terminating at my ankle. His idea was to straighten out my right foot a bit so that my body mechanics worked with me rather than against me.

It was a lot to think about. Despite being overweight and slow, I was managing with my body the way it was. I had found ways to help my body mostly keep up with me, even if I looked funny walking or running. However, the idea of straightening out my foot and avoiding issues with my back in later years was exciting.

It seemed like an easy decision, but I had to consider the fact that it meant I would have to re-learn to walk, deal with more full-leg casts and spend a much longer stretch in a wheelchair while the bone regrew. Then I would have to undergo physiotherapy again. Still, if the surgeon was correct, this would all be short-term grief in the big picture of my life.

7

My mother and I spoke at length about the surgery – what it would mean and the possibility of my being able to walk with less pain or my trademarked walking "wobble" that made it look like I was always in dire need of a toilet. It wasn't all that easy of a decision, but in the end my mother let me make the choice, as the surgery wasn't deemed necessary and I'd be the one suffering through the recovery.

That's a big decision for a 10-year-old. However, the surgeon was certain this surgery would eliminate a lot of my issues and prevent new ones from developing so I went ahead with his suggestion. I was quickly scheduled for my fourth and final surgery.

8

Looking back now I realize we should have gotten more information or at least asked about certain possible outcomes. Having had countless additional surgeries as an adult, none of which had anything to do with my leg or foot, I learned to question everything and get full clarification before a surgery. Now I need to know exactly what's going to happen. Then, I ask how necessary it really is. Live and learn, I suppose. Back then, however, I was only 10 and my mother had no reason to not trust the surgeon.

What hadn't been explained to us at the time was that the surgery also meant that my leg wouldn't be able to continue to grow muscle properly. I'd end up with what's called a 'stove-pipe' leg or in other words, a right leg that's about half the circumference of the left leg.

I guess the surgeon assumed that I wouldn't choose leg modeling as a possible career path but when someone has a clearly deformed limb, it's going to affect them in one way or another, especially if that person is a child. And it did affect me – or, rather, I let it affect me. Throughout my life and until I was in my mid-20s, I avoided shorts, changing in front of people and bathing suits at all costs. Much like my extra girth, I was embarrassed by my right leg and foot. It didn't help that people liked to stare at it. Not only did my leg stick out due to its small size, but the huge scar that ran from just below my knee to below my sock line didn't help.

Of course, I eventually grew out of that embarrassment, but not until I was much older and not until I had made my right, twisted and deformed leg look like the sexier of the two via a horrific accident involving my stupidity and a folding chair.

Looking back, it's impossible to know how things would have turned out had the surgeon waited a few years, allowing my body to finish growing and for my leg to put on some more muscle before cutting me open and filling my leg with metal. Honestly, though, I've grown to accept both of my legs completely. Now when someone glances down at them and does a double-take, I just smile and say, "Yep, shark attack."

9

Although I was told that the surgery had been a success, the recovery was brutal and seemed to drag on forever. I put on even more weight and my body didn't heal the way the doctors thought it would. What none of us realized at the time was that I was also dealing with Crohn's disease. This meant, among many other things, that my immune system was functioning at a crawl which in turned slowed down the healing process.

I wouldn't be diagnosed with Crohn's for another eight years so while I impatiently waited for my body to repair itself, I spent an even longer amount of time confined to a wheelchair while I packed on even more pounds.

10

Weeks of recovery slowly turned into months of recovery with plenty of casts, the need to relearn to walk on a rotated foot, physiotherapy and eventually crutches. When the last cast was finally removed, my leg still angled out a bit. However, my foot appeared to curve inwards even more, looking like a large, reversed letter C. I was mortified.

11

After I had gotten through the long recovery, the bone had regrown and I had learned to walk again, I went in for what I thought would be my final checkup with the surgeon. Although he was pleased that the leg had finally healed, he no longer called the surgery a success. My foot and leg would remain twisted, and he explained that he could not do anything more for me. I remember him apologizing like it was his fault or like he could have done more. However, I've never felt that way. Despite my being greatly bothered by how my right foot looked, walking was already easier than it had been before.

Before letting us go the surgeon went over the dos and don'ts, how to take care of my leg and foot, his recommendations for special orthotics and the like. Then, the word 'impossible' came out again. He gave me the same spiel I had heard so many times before: that I would always require special shoes, supports and canes. And of course, I would still end up dealing with pain and I could forget about any sport that included running.

My mother and I left his office, his words bouncing around in my head.

12

That word again, *impossible.* I had heard it way too much. It's a word reserved, in my opinion, for those who either want a way out of something or who aren't willing to fight hard enough for it.

I had no interest in that word and I never gave it much stock throughout most of my youth. Between surgeries I participated in every sport I could, even those that involved running. Of course, that was only when I wasn't on crutches or confined to a wheelchair – and unfortunately that was most of the time. However, when I was free of those contraptions, I played my heart out, hobbling around as best as I could. It may not have looked pretty, and I probably just served to help the opposing team, but I showed up with heart and my friends and classmates never once made fun of me.

Sadly, the word 'impossible' did eventually catch up with me but not until after that final surgery. Trying to adapt to my newly rotated foot and obesity took their toll. I found myself dealing with more pain than I was accustomed to and I started avoiding all physical activity. When I finally fell victim to that terrible word, I fell hard. That was only out of fear, and to be honest, it was my own fault. Good thing the words' hold over me was short-lived. Well, short-lived in dog years.

13

A few years after my recovery I was offered one last surgery, one that would mean removing the titanium rod and screws that were no longer deemed necessary to hold my leg together. I was excited to think that I'd have the opportunity to have two normal-looking legs again, but the doctors were quick to tell me that the muscle tissue would never grow the same. Hence, the surgery wouldn't technically add anything to my life.

That decision was left to me as well but making it was much easier. To this day, I set off metal detectors in airports around the world.

14

In the end, the doctors were partially right about requiring the special shoes, shoe lifts, orthotics, braces and the like. Where they were wrong was about how long I would need them … or, perhaps better put, how long I would actually use them. I subscribed to all those gadgets until I was in my mid-teens, then finally did away with them. I decided to stop relying on those things unless they were absolutely necessary, and none of them were. They may have helped but they seemed more trouble than they were worth. Plus, they slowed me down.

Today, I walk with a substantial limp and I run the same way. I don't notice either unless someone points them out to me. In the past, as I said, that bothered me greatly. Today, if someone points it out while I'm running and asks me why, I simply smile, take a moment to be grateful for what I'm able to do and then show them it's nothing at all by rocketing ahead of them, leaving them in a trail of dust.

Chapter 2 – My First First-Place Finish

I'm not entirely sure why but for some reason I spent very little time feeling sorry for myself. I'm guessing I learned this from my mother who raised five children on her own: a special needs child, one who constantly rebelled, a set of twins and then me. Yet, she never took a dime from any type of social assistance program nor ever complained. She was and still is a warrior yet kind-hearted and loving. I'm grateful for her gentle strength.

She taught me well. Even at a young age I was determined to make the most of my situation and not let it bring me down.

2

Shortly after my final surgery, and while I still needed a wheelchair due to the cast running from my toes to my groin, my school decided to put on a fundraiser for cancer research. It involved collecting pledges and then running laps around the school track.

I was very excited to be part of the fundraiser as my father had died of cancer when I was just 18 months old. However, being in a wheelchair with a full leg cast I knew my involvement would be altered. I wasn't in any shape to run laps but felt that perhaps I could somehow wheel myself around the school track. It was a pebble track that was brutal to maneuver on, but I felt that simply collecting pledges and not doing the gritty part wasn't right. Plus, I'd always wanted to be treated as equally as possible. I felt awkward when people had to bend the rules or system for me and my handicap.

With that in mind I approached my principal and explained how I wanted to get involved. He didn't see things the same way and insisted that I could be associated with only the fundraising portion of the event.

I explained to him that the fundraiser involved more than just collecting money from people. It involved running for that money. I didn't want special treatment. I didn't want to be only partially included. I wanted to collect money and run just like my friends and classmates would, but in a wheelchair. I assured him that I would do so without help from anyone pushing me and that I wouldn't block the track. I could wheel myself around the track before and after school when no one else was around.

He didn't seem to appreciate my concerns or desires and refused to budge, saying that the fundraiser was about running around a track, not wheeling around a track.

I was heartbroken.

3

I never knew my father, at least not that I can recall. I was simply too young to remember. He died well before his prime, at only 31 years of age. However, that didn't mean I didn't care or that I'd simply give in to a bully of a principal. I wanted to honor my father and I wanted to show that principal that I could be involved and participate like my friends. Plus, I really wanted the challenge, to push myself. I'd spent most of my childhood unable to do basic things and now I had an opportunity to do something really big – at least to me. I couldn't tell you why I felt that way or why I was so disappointed about being excluded from part of the fundraiser. I only knew that I felt it absolutely necessary to be involved as completely as possible.

4

By the time classes ended that day, I had developed a rough plan. I'd been in the wheelchair for far too long this time around as I was afraid to upgrade to crutches due to the pain from my heavy cast pulling on my leg. I had this crazy kid notion that my foot would be pulled right off my leg if the bone hadn't regrown, or something along those lines.

I needed a push to get over my fear and to start building strength in my right leg. I felt that this was my opportunity. The burning desire to get myself around that school track, make money for cancer research and prove my principal wrong far outweighed my fear or pain.

I wheeled home as quickly as possible, desperate to share my plan with my mother. It was a simple plan in theory but would take some physical strength on my end, possibly some manipulation of my sisters (which I admit I was getting good at by then) and a plan to conquer our little town of 4,000.

5

When my mother came home from work, I explained that I wanted to get back onto the crutches so that I could 'run' laps around the school track. I would need my sisters' help getting to and from school, both before and after classes, as I didn't want my principal to see me.

She thought it was a great idea, supported me fully and went to work filing down the top of my cast so my leg would be able to swing more freely. I then spoke with my sisters who didn't need any type of manipulation at all – they were both keen to help their little brother.

6

My sisters took turns pushing my wheelchair around our neighborhood, stopping at every house and chatting with our neighbors about the fundraiser. I sat at the bottom of their front stairs in my wheelchair, looking sad and helpless, my large cast in plain sight.

My sisters explained that their little brother, whose father had died of cancer when he was just a baby, was going to 'run' laps around the school track to raise money for cancer. They explained that I would be doing so on crutches.

Our neighbors, already knowing my story from having known me for years, looked down at me while I looked up at them, my little heart seemingly broken, trying a pathetic smile to show that everything was OK – that I was a little trooper and simply wanted to be part of the fundraiser when I was the only child in my class who had lost a parent to cancer.

It was brilliant even though it was also complete manipulation.

7

The school had offered donors two options: a

pledge per lap or a one-time, single donation. Single donations were fine, but the big money was in the pledge per lap. I knew this and I obviously wanted to raise as much money as possible. I also had a secret goal - one I'm sure all my friends had - of raising more than anyone else at school. Of course, I also secretly fantasized that I would "outrun" everyone else, but I knew that was a very lofty goal and almost certainly not going to happen.

My sisters emphasized to our neighbors that, with my cast, it would be extremely difficult for me to get around the track. I would not be able to accept help and I could count only the laps I completed on my own.

I had my sisters explain that although a single donation would be very much appreciated, we were really aiming for per-lap pledges.

8

Wanting to do right by the boy in the wheelchair who had lost his father to the very disease for which he was now raising money, our generous neighbors mostly pledged per lap. Some of those pledges were shockingly high. So high in fact that I assumed it was going to be difficult to get everyone to pay up, assuming I could get around that track enough times.

The pledge collecting went so well on our first day that we decided to hit up a second neighborhood. The next day, we went out again, hitting up yet another neighborhood, then another. Day after day, we went out and conquered more and more parts of town. We kept at it until we hit every single neighborhood and we were absolutely exhausted.

9

My sisters had worked tirelessly, lifting me into our mother's car, loading the wheelchair into the trunk, driving me across town, then unloading me and wheeling me from door to door in as many neighborhoods as the day would permit. They rang the doorbells of the wealthy, the not-so-wealthy and everyone in between. I practiced my "sad but brave" face and people pledged.

We collected an insane number of pledges and I only hoped that I could keep up my end of the bargain. Soon I would have to start hobbling around the track. I had no idea whether my leg could handle the weight of the cast, the swinging and the stress on the metal rod in my leg.

This, of course, was key. All the fundraising we did and all the pledges we collected would be for naught if I couldn't get around that track.

10

The day finally came. Everyone was to start running laps during recess and at lunch and I decided that I wanted to be there with them. I felt that I no longer had to run laps before and after school, hidden from the teachers, since I wasn't in my wheelchair. I was excited and proud and I wanted to participate with my friends.

I also was very interested in seeing how many laps my friends were going to run. With all the pledges I had collected, I was hell-bent on beating everyone in the money-collecting portion of the process. I had come to my senses and realized that there was no way I could beat them in laps, but I was still curious about how they would do. And on some level, I really thought that I could beat at least a few of my friends in total laps. That would be a huge victory for me and give me some bragging rights.

One of my teachers officially started us off and away we went, my friends leaving me in a cloud of dust and dirt. I hobbled my way around the track, taking breaks every few meters or so. While I rested on my crutches my friends and classmates were lapping me, getting in five or six laps for every lap I managed. However, I didn't feel disheartened.

What I did feel was pain. My leg and hip ached something fierce and my cast was hot, making my leg sweat and itch. Meanwhile, my armpits burned from the constant pressure and friction from the crutches, and my fresh scar, that ran the length of my leg, seemed to beat along with my heart.

When that first recess ended, I don't think I made it around the track more than three times, and maybe less. I have no idea how many laps my friends did but it seemed like a lot. I was passed over constantly, but no one ever made fun of me. Instead, all I recall were words of praise and slaps on the back.

Best of all, my principal was nowhere to be seen. I could only hope it stayed that way. Unfortunately, my hopes were short-lived.

11

When the school bell rang, I slowly made my way back to class, worn out and wincing but happy to have completed a couple of laps. I had barely seated myself before I heard my name over the school intercom. My presence was requested in the principal's office.

I was fairly certain why I was being beckoned. My heart raced in my chest once more. When I arrived at his office, I plunked myself down into a chair, grateful to be off the crutches again despite where I was.

My principal looked me over, surely noticing how sweaty I was from having hobbled around the school track in the heat. His face started glowing bright red which was his tell that he was about to explode. It was common knowledge to basically everyone in the school as we saw it often and it never ended well.

Being the adventurous child I was, I had the misfortune of seeing that red face far too many times. I could tell then, sitting uncomfortably across from him with my crutches leaning against the chair, that his face was about to light up like never before.

I honestly don't recall what he yelled at me, but he definitely made it clear that I was to stop running around the track on my crutches and immediately. He reminded me that I was permitted to fundraise and that was all. Nothing more.

I left his office feeling heartbroken but also more determined than ever.

I made my way home that day and told my mother and sisters what had happened. After a brief conversation we decided to revert to our plan of having one of my sisters drive me to school early in the morning and before any of the teachers showed up. Then the other would drive me back to school once everyone was gone for the day. I was going to run those laps and there was no way was I going to let my power-tripping principal stop me. We would keep track of my laps and deal with submitting them when that time came. I was a dog with a bone. I had something big to prove to my principal, but more importantly, to myself. And honestly, I couldn't have cared less about what he thought I should and shouldn't be doing on my own time.

12

The very next day we put our plan into motion. I was excruciatingly slow at first and I'm not sure how my sisters found the patience to deal with me for the first few weeks. However, slowly my body strengthened and my leg seemed to either heal or accept the abuse I was inflicting on it.

I hobbled around that track faster and faster. Eventually, I felt as if I were flying. On days when it rained, my sisters would tie plastic garbage bags over my cast, then stand under an umbrella, still counting and making sure it was all official. On days when the sun shined, they speed walked beside me and kept me company, laughing and taking my mind off the blisters that would form, pop, harden and reform in my armpits from the crutches.

Eventually, my mother sewed small, special pillows and attached them to the hardened foam cushions at the top of the crutches. This allowed me to hobble with less pain.

My sisters and mother worked hard to turn those days into memories I will never forget.

When I eventually went back to my neighbors to collect on their pledges, it turned out to be a day they wouldn't forget, either.

13

I can partially recall being a little embarrassed to go back to each house and ask for the money I had earned through the pledges. Some people put up a bit of a fight, thinking they had been taken. Others refused to pay. And others yet decided to change their pledge from per-lap to a one-time pledge. However, mostly the people paid up as promised. We assured them that I hadn't cheated them out of a single lap and we had the lap count sheets at the ready.

Though not everyone paid up, and some chose to pay less, in the end I had collected over a couple thousand dollars in pledges, and that was back in 1985.

14

From talking to a few of my friends, it seemed like I had raised substantially more than they did, but I really didn't know how I stacked up overall. I also had no idea how well I'd done against them as far as the number of laps were concerned; I was too afraid to ask my friends how many they'd gotten in.

The day we started running laps, everyone was constantly lapping me. However, from Day 2 onwards I'd run on my own. In the end I knew I had logged an incredible number of laps, especially considering the circumstances, and that I should have been proud of my achievements. However, I was a kid and the school had prizes for both laps run and money raised so I was interested mostly in the prizes – and, of course, the fame that went with winning.

Throughout the process I had been submitting my donation sheets to my teacher but held back my lap sheets. I didn't want to catch hell from the principal again. However, once the fundraiser came to an end, I snuck my count sheets into the pile along with everyone else's, hoping I wouldn't be seen.

Clearly, I hadn't thought it through completely as my secret would no longer be between my sisters, my mother and I. I suppose I thought that once my principal saw the dedication and effort I'd put into the fundraiser, his heart of stone would magically change.

Whatever it was I'd thought or hoped for, I was about to be disappointed. Again.

15

Judgement day came and every single student in the entire school and all the teachers gathered in the gym, eagerly awaiting the results. We wanted to know who had raised the most money and completed the most laps and the room was abuzz.

The principal took the podium, shushed the room and started by reading the names of the top fundraisers.

I held my breath while he called out the third-place fundraiser who had raised substantially less than I had. This meant I was guaranteed to take either first or second place.

When he called out the next name for the second highest fundraiser, and it wasn't mine, I was thrilled but not overly surprised. My family and I had worked incredibly hard collecting pledges over the course of a few weeks.

When he finally called my name for most money raised, I proudly hobbled to the front of the gym and collected my ribbon, then hobbled back to my place. I felt extremely happy to have raised so much for a charity that was important to me. Deep down, however, I also really wanted to win the prize for the most laps run. As hard as I had worked to raise money, I had poured literal blood, sweat and tears into those laps and had never worked so hard at anything in my life. Leaning on my crutches in that auditorium, after all that hard work, I no longer thought it an impossibility to place in the top three.

16

Our school principal shuffled some papers, then prepared to announce the three students who had completed the most laps. I held my breath as he called out the third-place finisher and the laps that student had completed.

Despite having a secret goal to crush some of my friends and classmates on laps completed, I still had a nagging voice in the back of my head that told me it would be impossible to have done so under the circumstances. However, when I heard the number of laps that the third-place finisher had completed, and I realized that this person had run substantially fewer laps than I had, I was beside myself. Once again, I knew I had placed either second or first. I was excited beyond words and quite shocked.

I no longer cared if I took first or second place; I was ecstatic enough to be in the top three.

There was a stir of excitement in the gym and the principal hushed the room once more. Everyone waited for him to announce the second-place finisher and the laps completed.

After what seemed like an eternity, he slowly spoke the next name. It wasn't mine.

I could hardly believe it! Not only had I raised the most money, but I had also completed the most laps around the school track, and by far. And I did it all on crutches and with a cast! I was very proud of myself and immediately started hobbling towards the front of the gym before he called my name.

I was nearing the front of the gym, smiling from ear to ear and heading towards the podium for a second time when he shuffled his papers one last time and called out the last name. The name he called wasn't mine.

17

I must have gone a hundred shades of red, standing there in front of my entire school, beaming like I'd won while one of my classmates ran past me to collect their award.

I suppose I should have known on some level that the principal wouldn't count my laps as he had made it very clear to me that he wouldn't, but I guess I thought he'd somehow come around.

I quickly turned around and hobbled towards the back of the gymnasium as fast as I could. I pushed my way through the double doors and into the hallway. I was confused, embarrassed, heartbroken and utterly defeated.

Rather than going back to class, I hobbled straight home.

18

My mother is a soft-spoken, gentle woman who rarely gets angry, but when I told her the story, I thought her head was going to pop off. While I begged her to not do so, she drove me directly to the school, burst into the principal's office and then threatened all types of horrific and horrendous things. She also demanded an apology and my award.

I'm not sure who was more embarrassed, my principal or me. We both sat there with our heads hung in shame.

I got that apology there on the spot and the next day my name was announced over the school's intercom as being the person who had not only collected the most pledges but also run the most laps.

A day or so later, I received my first first-place ribbon and hung it with extreme pride in my bedroom.

Chapter 3 – House of Cards

I may have started my life of running early and with an epic charity challenge, however, that was the end of my 'running' and tackling big physical challenges for the next 15 years. It was the word *impossible* that I fell victim to, and again, I can blame only myself. That word can be a vicious trap.

Perhaps I had graduated to crutches early due to the fundraiser, but I also continued using them for far longer than expected as my leg just wasn't healing the way it was supposed to. Perhaps the added stress of having an early-80s model, multi-pound cast pulling on my leg for a few hundred laps around the school track hadn't done it any favors. I experienced a lot of pain and it seemed to take forever before I was able to put weight on that foot and leg after the cast was removed. That pain led to fear, which opened the door to that word: 'impossible.' I like to think that I fought it for a while, but eventually I lost that initial energy and drive. I fell victim to the words of my doctors and specialists and to my own doubts that I could actually do more than the limits they'd set for me.

2

I became more lethargic and the weight continued to pack on. I was also going through puberty and everything involved with that but without the ability to get outside and burn off the extra testosterone and hormones. Instead, I fell into a bit of a depression without even realizing it. I found comfort in food, but unfortunately not the healthy stuff. I went from being a pudgy kid to very obese.

3

Depression and weight gain can create a slippery slope – one from which it's very hard to recover, especially when you don't realize you're depressed. In my case, the depression was worsened by the fact that Crohn's disease prevents the body from producing enough serotonin, known as the body's naturally produced 'happy drug.'

It was a vicious cycle of eating, being in pain from eating due to Crohn's disease, being depressed and wanting to eat more, finding momentary yet false happiness in food and then once again dealing with the pain from eating. All the while I spent a ridiculous amount of time in the washroom yet had no idea why as I had yet to be diagnosed with Crohn's.

Of course, my entire childhood can't be summed up like that. There were definitely more good times than bad ones, but when the depression did take hold, its grip was fierce.

4

My adolescence slowly slipped away as did my early teens. I found myself edging closer to both adulthood and 200 pounds, with plenty of self-image issues. I constantly had stomach issues and pain and all the confidence I'd had while growing up, despite what I went through, faded over the next few years. On the inside I felt lost, pathetic and helpless to change. Fortunately, on the outside I still managed to exude confidence, even at my weakest moments. At the time I thought this was a blessing but now I'm not so sure.

Just like the garbage I was putting into my body and calling food, those negative words that I believed about my body and health were also garbage. I just hadn't realized it yet.

I slowly became an angry, dispassionate and short-tempered person whom I didn't know or understand. I projected my blame outwards; this became my coping strategy. Rather than working to better myself as a person, finding a medical solution and dealing with my problems properly, I focused on a new job that quickly evolved into a 10-year career.

5

I was 18 and living with my girlfriend, working a ridiculous number of hours in the hopes of shedding my poor roots. All the while I was continuing to abuse my body at an alarming rate. I wasn't into alcohol or drugs but my unhealthy love of sweets, deep-fried awesomeness and junk food in general was destructive enough. I was making more money than I knew what to do with and therefore felt that I could afford to eat out whenever I wanted. And I did. Being barely 18 with deep pockets, I consumed almost every meal in a restaurant.

Being six-foot-one allowed me to hide some of my additional girth for a while by using the right clothing. However, I couldn't escape the damage to my health and self-esteem.

6

Another handful of years passed and my girlfriend became my wife and our careers blossomed. We climbed the corporate ladder at the same time and with great success, becoming highly paid regional managers for one of Canada's largest employers.

I had been promoted to a position as the company's youngest-ever manager and then as the company's youngest-ever regional manager. Together, my wife and I made an obscene amount of money and we were only in our early 20s.

With each new promotion the number of hours required at work increased substantially until I was working between 80 and 110 hours a week. Between working around the clock and the fact that I spent much of my time out of town and sleeping in hotels, my health took a further hit as did the scale beneath my feet.

I thought that we were living the dream, holding prestigious positions, raking in large bonuses, going on five-star vacations and buying whatever we wanted, whenever we wanted. And I think that in many people's eyes we *were* living the dream. However, looks can be deceiving. The truth was only a few steps behind us and catching up quickly.

Everything in my life was coming to a head. Unbeknownst to me, I was quickly approaching my midlife crisis at the quarter-life age of 25. My tipping point was just barely ahead on the horizon though I thought I was riding the wave of success and achievement.

The straw that broke the camel's back was a full-blown Crohn's attack. Although it was a horrific experience (and not just for the actual attack), it – like the problems with my leg and foot – turned out to be a major blessing in disguise.

Chapter 4 – Gut Check

My mother had assumed that I had Crohn's disease from around the time of my 10th birthday, but every time she took me to the hospital with severe stomach pain, the doctors refused to test me saying that Crohn's was reserved for the elderly. To their credit, they didn't want to submit a child to the testing required and honestly, I'm grateful. That's not because I didn't go through those horrible exams to find out that I was indeed afflicted with the disease, but because they surely would have put me on medication even earlier than I ended up having to start it.

In the end, I dealt with the constant pain, bloating, diarrhea, constipation and the rest by continuing down the path of poor food choices and ignorance until I was almost into my 20s.

2
Somewhere between my 18th and 19th birthday I had experienced my first Crohn's attack. Attacks range from searing stomach and side pain to complete incapacitation with pain and the need for immediate medical care. I had experienced many issues over the years but nothing like this first full-blown attack. It was as

if someone was repeatedly stabbing me in my side and taking a full breath was almost impossible. It was horrifying. It was also to be only the first major attack of many over the following decade or so.

My wife had still been my girlfriend at the time and she had rushed me to the hospital. I was expecting - or perhaps hoping - that I would receive some heavy-duty pain killers as per usual, then sent home to properly recover. Instead, I spent the next week in the hospital while they submitted me to a barrage of tests before diagnosing me with Crohn's. Then they put me on an incredible diet of pills.

3

Crohn's is an auto-immune disease that attacks either the small or large intestine and creates a laundry list of secondary effects like dead intestine, anal abscesses, anal bleeding, excruciating pain, the need to have parts of the colon and/or intestines removed (which can lead to the need for a colostomy bag) and many more equally exciting and sexy problems. It's also known to increase the odds of cancer in its victims.

After my diagnosis I was put in touch with a dietician who simply told me what not to eat, said that the disease was not curable and indicated that very little was known about the causes. I glanced over the black-listed foods which read like a menu at my favorite restaurant: sweets, cheese, greasy foods, dairy, popcorn, nuts, seeds, alcohol, tobacco, soft drinks, raw vegetables and much more.

I'd like to tell you that I gave it my all and religiously followed the dietician's suggestions, but using her own words, not much was known about the cause of the disease. Therefore, I thought that perhaps they were wrong about what to put on that list of banned foods. Simple arrogance and ignorance neatly wrapped together on my part.

Instead of following the dietician's advice completely, I decided to partially follow it and continued my habit of avoiding raw vegetables. Well, actually all vegetables, but just to be safe.

4

Other than the usual searing gut pain for a couple of hours after every meal, constant inflammation that made me look pregnant most of the time and a chronic abscess high on my backside, I dealt with the disease pretty well. I had more flare-ups or mini attacks and more of the full-blown ones, but I was already used to the hospital visits. The only adjustment I had to make was to become accustomed to the internal scopes and fingers in places where I didn't want them to be.

I stuck to the regimen of popping prescribed pills then eventually graduated to intramuscular injections. All the while the disease progressed and the secondary effects of the medication did their damage – in some cases, permanent damage.

Against doctor's orders I continued eating everything I was told not to eat and I avoided exercise due to my work schedule and dislike for it at the time. My condition slowly worsened during the years that took me from a stock boy to a highly paid regional manager and from single to married, until the day my wife found me passed out naked on the bathroom floor after work.

5

For the next couple of years after that first attack, I had been doing my best to ignore the disease and the pain that went with it. That wasn't easy, however, as the pain was constant as were the cramps, diarrhea and that recurring abscess. Due to constant inflammation, my right side almost always protruded as if I had a hernia. Considering my girth at the time, it didn't look all that out of place. Still, it felt like I'd eaten a football.

I eventually learned to avoid some foods that created the most issues for me, but really, I was barely making it through each day. Other days it got so bad I was throwing up because of the pain and the fact that my stomach was rejecting a lot of the food I consumed.

My health continued to deteriorate while I focused on my career and everything else other than my health until the day it all came to a head.

I had come home early, sick with incredible abdominal pain. I remember stripping down naked as even the fabric of my clothes touching my stomach had been unbearable. Then, at some point, I had apparently been trying to crawl to the toilet as I could no longer walk. The pain was so intense I blacked out on the way there.

It's not how anyone would want to be found and it's worse when you consider that the person finding you probably thinks you're dead. I can only imagine the horror of finding someone you care about like that.

As bad as that must have been for my tiny wife, and after the initial relief of realizing that I wasn't dead, she would have discovered that she had to somehow dress all 250 pounds of me and then carry me out to the car. I was more than double her size. To this day, I have no idea how she managed to do it or why she didn't just call an ambulance, but I'll always be grateful.

6

My (our) horrific experience should have been a painful wakeup call, one that I desperately needed. However, I was still young and clearly very ignorant. I was too focused on my career and put all my chips into that basket. Instead of using that incident to create positive and necessary change in my life, I was pumped full of drugs and sent home to recover. I headed back to work the next day.

Although it was the first and last time I passed out from pain, I had been spending the previous five or six years in and out of the hospital for Crohn's attacks. Each time my doctor reprimanded me for not taking better care of my health.

I had been caught in a terrible cycle of working too hard, making more money, being promoted and then getting sick. Each time I got sick, which had become more frequent, I tried harder to push my health aside and focus more on my career.

That terrible cycle continued until I finally woke up and realized that I was trying to avoid the unavoidable. I had been living in denial, focusing more on the day-to-day of my job so that I didn't have to face the truth about two major issues that I was faced with at that time. Neither had anything to do with my physical health but both everything to do with my mental and emotional health.

I had been burying my head in the sand, slogging away at life pretending that everything was amazing. Big, beautiful house, gorgeous wife, impressive position with a major company, lavish toys and vacations and everything else. What I was trying to avoid seeing was that I was in a failing marriage and my career - which I was working so hard at - was actually killing me.

I had reached my tipping point and it was time to change. The only thing was, I wasn't sure how. By then my wife and I were both in the middle of the race to the top of the retail ladder, neck deep in our careers and ignorantly focused on 'living the dream.' We had pushed everything else to the bottom of our list of priorities. Hence, we weren't capable of properly dealing with my failing health at the time.

Yet I somehow knew that I had to make major changes in both my personal life and professional life. I had enough sense to realize that the stress in my life contributed majorly to my failing health.

7

I had spent a huge chunk of my early life living in some sort of bubble that didn't accommodate reasoning or rational thought. I was blinded by success at my work, by the possessions I was able to buy after having grown up very poor and by following the recipe that so many claim is the best way to live your life: study hard, get a good job, get married, buy a house, have children, pay your taxes, enjoy the handful of hours on the weekends (if you're somehow able to avoid work emails and phone calls), retire when you're too old to enjoy doing anything and then die, supposedly fulfilled.

Sadly, that recipe doesn't focus on health, happiness or true success in life; it focuses only on perceived success. It does, however, lead to stress and for me, disease.

8

I woke up in the hospital yet again and after another Crohn's attack. My doctor was at my side, explaining what was going on. Essentially, my body was killing itself from the inside out. He told me what my future would look like if I didn't make real and immediate changes and then told me that surgery was now necessary.

He told me he wanted to remove parts of my colon and intestine and then give me a colostomy bag. He talked about the increased possibility of cancer, something that had taken both of my grandfathers and my father. He went on and on while I zoned out. I'd heard enough after the first minute.

The experience of sitting in that hospital bed, listening to my doctor spin a horror story was enough to finally push me to my tipping point and in grand fashion. Thinking back, I'm embarrassed that it took such a wake-up call to create the much-needed change in my life.

9

For years I had felt that I was living someone else's life, blindly following the praise of friends, family and coworkers for all I had achieved by the young age of 25. Yet despite the money, respect and power I felt empty, shallow and lost. And of course, there was my failing health.

My relationship had continued to deteriorate as well and most likely at the same rate as my health. Unlike my health, however, we both worked to solve our relationship issues though we were getting nowhere fast. At the time she had subscribed to that boxed perception of success whereas I sought something more enriching, even if I didn't know what that looked like at the time.

While in the hospital and after my doctor finished giving me the news, I accepted that I had to make some major changes in my life or reboot it entirely. That meant creating a huge shift in focus which would undeniably take me way out of my comfort zone. The question was, was I ready for that shift and change?

10

That particular time I spent two weeks in the hospital while my doctor ran test after test and while my body slowly recovered. Against my doctor's wishes, I managed to refuse the surgery and kept my intestines and colon intact. I don't recall ever being so ill but my time in the hospital was exactly what I needed. It was the first real break I'd had since starting full-time work at the age of 11. It was a blessing in many ways, not the least of which was that it gave me time to think about what I had to do with my life.

I realized that the four biggest areas of concern that needed immediate attention were: my career, my relationship, my health and my happiness. And not necessarily in that order.

I also realized that I could start making changes immediately but that none of the changes would be pleasant or easy. Quitting my job, as fun as that would be, meant not being able to pay my mortgage. Finding a new job meant taking what I assumed would be a serious pay cut. Getting healthy would be a long, arduous road and especially considering that I was at my all-time high of 252 pounds. Efforts to fix my marriage had been a major focus for the two or three years leading up to this awakening yet were yielding nothing. Most likely this meant it was already over, just not officially. As for my personal happiness, well, what did that look like? I had grown up extremely poor and had nothing but had been happier than when I'd had everything I could possibly want.

I had some big decisions to make and they seemed overwhelming at the time. I'd clearly made a wrong turn somewhere between trying to find happiness through my bank account and accumulating a bunch of possessions I never had time to enjoy. It was time for corrective action. It was a lot to think about and especially considering that I was going to have to deal with it on my own, which scared me half to death.

It was then that I started thinking about my father and how he'd died at 31. He was just barely getting going at life when we lost him. And everything he'd achieved, also by a very young age, no longer mattered. I started to realize that my prestigious job, my bank account, quarterly bonus and all the furniture and toys in my over-sized house meant nothing if I was going to die young as well – and worse if it was at my own hands.

It started to click for me then, as I lay in that hospital bed all alone. I vowed to change. It didn't matter how difficult that change was going to be. Anything beat the path I'd been on and tough change definitely trumped death.

PART II

Taking Responsibility

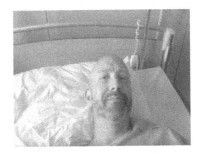

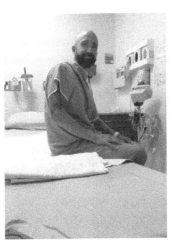

Chapter 5 – A Bathroom Miracle

I was barely home from my last stint in the hospital and still very conscious of the idea that I had to change but was simply spinning my tires. Knowing you need to change and pulling the trigger are two very different things. I was definitely wanting the change and very open to ideas about how to go about making that change, but I needed help or some sort of inspiration to fall into my lap. And then, just like that, it did.

2

I had been settling in to enjoy some of my 'Crohn's-induced bathroom time' at work one day when I realized that I forgot my book at home. Fortunately, a tattered magazine was sitting on the back of the toilet. Flipping through it I came across the inspiration that I desperately needed in the form of a Martin Luther King Jr quote. That quote, 'If You Can't Fly, Then Run' started the wheels of change in ways I would never have believed. It was a powerful quote but one that had nothing to do with running nor exercise in general, just about pushing forward no matter what.

3

I had been dealing with foot and leg issues all my life – painful issues that I thought had prevented me from doing more. Yet, I had been spending upwards of 16 hours a day on my feet every day at work. I'm sure I easily averaged 15 kilometers a day or more. So then, I thought, why couldn't I run? What was the difference? Just a little speed, right?

It was so profound for me, it was like someone had hit me hard with my own bag of excuses.

I can't tell you why, but I'd always wanted to run. Perhaps it was because I was told that I couldn't or perhaps because we humans are designed to run, not walk. Regardless, it was like I'd been shackled for the past 15 years and someone had just handed me the key.

Up to that moment my life had been in absolute turmoil. I felt stuck beyond measure. All those major issues had immobilized me, or so it felt. Then, just like that, I felt a huge sense of relief. The quote hadn't just pointed out the obvious; it had reminded me that I was in charge of my life and always had been. Somewhere along the line I had forgotten and had given up my personal power. My problems, as big as they were, were not bigger than I was nor greater than my ability to conquer them. I simply had to get moving. And that's exactly what I did.

Chapter 6 – Turning a Disability into an Ability

Those powerful words that I had read had given me hope and fired me up in almost inexplicable ways. It woke something deep in me that had been lying dormant for far too long and that was ready to be unleashed. Such a simple thing but the timing apparently was perfect and exactly what I needed. I couldn't wait to leave work that day, rush home and gear up. This new-found energy couldn't have come at a better time. I was certain that it would be the first step in creating monumental change in my life. I knew it would because for years leading up that point, I had felt that I wanted to run away from everything in my life, though at the time I thought just metaphorically speaking.

2

I drove home from work with this new-found energy and excitement for positive change.

When I finally arrived, I burst through the front door of my house and barely acknowledged my wife before hitting her with a barrage of questions.

"Where are my running shoes? Do I own running shoes? How about my gym shorts? Did you throw away all of my ripped T-shirts? Do you think I can run in my khaki shorts?"

I think I threw her off. While she was accustomed to me bursting into our home with a barrage of questions, typically they were questions about dinner, not running.

"What are you up to? Finally painting the garage?" Her sarcasm was just her way of trying to annoy me.

"Never mind," I mumbled while running up the stairs to our bedroom, huffing and puffing as I did.

I managed to throw on some sort of outfit, had a quick glance at my very pudgy body in the mirror and was back downstairs and out the door within minutes of getting home. I knew that I had to get running before I changed my mind.

3

My biggest concern that day should have been my heart and how it would take this hasty decision to start running after years of abuse. Or, perhaps how my right foot and leg would respond. Instead, I was worried about what my neighbors would think.

I decided that I would have to make it look like it wasn't my first time running, just the first time they'd seen me running.

I hit the end of my front driveway at a run, swung to the right and ran past the first two houses on the block. Then I rounded the corner onto the main road and picked it up a couple of notches.

It felt amazing to be running. I realized that I was doing something that I'd been told was impossible for me. Yes, it felt awkward and I'm sure I looked very funny due to my strange gait, but my leg wasn't bothering me, my foot was fine, and I was actually running! The only question was, why hadn't I started doing this earlier? Well, that and whether my neighbors saw the cloud of dust I threw up burning past their houses!

4

This new-found energy was amazing! My legs were moving me faster than I thought possible. I pumped my arms and grinned from ear to ear! I was actually doing it and I started to forget what my neighbors thought! I was a machine and   there   was   no   stopping   me.

Well, at least not for those first 100 meters.

I came to the first crossroad that led into the next cul-de-sac. That was when I started realizing that my heart was potentially running faster than I was. I was also pretty sure I hadn't taken a single breath since leaving the house. Probably because I was trying to suck in my large gut.

I went from thinking that I'd just slow it down a bit to coming to a screeching halt within the next 10 meters. I honestly felt that my heart was going to beat itself out of my chest. My legs were burning and I was a sweaty mess despite the fact that I was almost still in the shadow of my own house. I was devastated and beaten.

I'd run just a touch more than one block and I honestly thought I was going to have a heart attack right there on the street in front of all my nosey neighbors.

5

I sat on an electrical box in the greenspace between the sidewalk and the road, waiting for my heart to slow down. I was utterly defeated, both physically and emotionally. I had set out with such high hopes and expectations but clearly those expectations were set way too high. I hadn't considered that the last time I'd run was over a decade and a half earlier and before putting on about 150 pounds.

When my heart had slowed to a mere 300 beats per minute, I dragged myself off the electrical box and headed home, slowly and with my head down. I no longer cared what my neighbors thought of my three-minute run, or the fact that I'd spent two of those minutes sitting. All I cared about was getting home and not dying on the sidewalk.

6

I pushed my way through the front door, stumbled the 10 steps into the living room and crashed to the floor in a heap. My wife came running over to see what had happened, then started laughing once she realized that I most likely wasn't going to die.

"Need me to call you an ambulance?" she mocked, laughing even harder.

I told her I didn't, but the truth was, I honestly thought it might have been necessary. Instead, I waited for my heart to slow even more. When it did, about 15 minutes later, I dragged myself upstairs for a hot shower and a sulk.

7

The next day at work was business as usual. A long, hard day full of stress, unruly customers and staff. It grated on me like all days at work.

Then I found my mind drifting back to the idea of running and I felt a little better.

Just the mere thought of going for a run somehow made the day a little more bearable. I wasn't thinking about how terrible my first run had been the previous day. Rather, I focused on the idea that I did something that I'd previously thought impossible, and that it was basically pain free. That keyed me up and made me smile.

I rushed home from work in a huff again, put on my running clothes and shoes, then headed straight for the door. My wife caught me before I could sneak out and asked, bewildered, if I was really going to try again.

I'm not sure who was more surprised; her, wondering why I hadn't remembered how close to death I'd come the day before, or me, for wanting to punish myself more. Either way, I gave her a smile that said I was tougher than she thought I was, then headed out the front door.

8

I was no longer concerned about my neighbors or how I looked. Instead, I considered my heart. I wanted to run, was going to run, but had to ensure I didn't kill myself in the process. I decided to start a little slower, spending the first block warming up and then speeding up for the second block onwards.

It was a simple plan and, in hindsight, not the greatest one but it's all I had at the time and I went with it.

When I reached the end of my driveway, I headed right once more but at a jogging pace. I puttered past the two houses again on the way to my street corner, then rounded the bend. This time, I held myself back from speeding up. I kept my slow, jogging pace and noticed that I felt considerably better than I had the previous day.

I kept it at half-speed until I reached the end of the street, then crossed the intersection to the next block, where I had tanked the day previous. I picked up my pace to a run.

9

It wasn't lost on me that I was already ahead of where I'd almost died the previous day. I noted the electrical box where I had rested, spat at it and then kept running. *Not today!* I thought.

Once more I could feel the power within me as I sped down the street, feeling unstoppable and like a well-oiled machine. Well, a well-fed machine if nothing else.

I kept up my unrealistic pace that second block, passing houses and seeing the start of the third block approaching quickly. I felt great but at the same time I started becoming aware of my heart again. It seemed that it, too, was racing and now out of control.

I'd barely made it to the end of the second block when, once more, the run had beat me. I was done.

10

There was another electrical box for me to sit on while I caught my breath. As I sat there, trying not to die again, I had a wonderful thought: *I just ran double what I ran the previous day!*

Sure, it was only 200 meters in total, but the point was that I'd run double! Double! And I felt exactly the same … absolutely terrible and perhaps in need of CPR … but I'd run double the distance!

I gave myself a couple minutes to sit there before I hauled myself back home, clambered up my front steps, pushed my way through the front door and into my living room and crashed onto the floor once more, this time with a smile of achievement.

My wife made a repeat performance of the previous night, joking about my needing an ambulance, but I shrugged it off. She wouldn't understand my personal victory, but I did. I laid there and relished the thought of my new personal best as well as the fact that I was sweating all over the carpet that my wife loved so much.

11

The next day at work I could hardly contain myself. I spent the entire day thinking about running and how I could best my last run. Could I double it again and run four blocks? I wasn't sure but that became my new goal.

Once I set that goal, I tried to focus on my work but found my mind repeatedly returning to running. It was crazy! I had just started running - if you could call it that - and it was already becoming an obsession.

After I set my goal, I don't think an hour had gone by before I started wondering if I could run farther than four blocks. It was perhaps unlikely, but I also didn't want to limit myself; I had been limited enough over the years.

Can my right leg and foot handle it? I wondered. *My lungs? Most importantly, my heart?*

So far, I hadn't experienced any pain in my leg and foot, but then again, I'd only run a total of 300 meters in two days. Well, OK, a total of 300 meters in 15 years assuming I didn't count all the times Crohn's made me run to a toilet.

The more I thought about it the more I believed my entire body could handle the extra distance as long as my heart could. That was the only real concern, but it was a big one!

I started thinking about my first two runs and how I'd been breathing rather hard, sounding like a freight train on a steep incline. It seemed that I couldn't catch my breath while running so I wondered what would happen if I had slowed down and held a jogging pace for longer or for the entire run? I didn't like the idea of running slowly but I had to consider whether the point was to run fast and end quickly or to take it slower and run farther?

The answer was obvious.

12

Rather than rushing straight home after work that day I made a quick stop at a bike store. I was determined to not only run more than the original four-block goal, but to run at least a full kilometer. It was a lofty goal, all things considered, but I wanted to attempt it. Because I had no idea how far a kilometer was in my neighborhood, and having an intense Type-A personality, I had to know exactly where that one-kilometer mark was. Hence, my purchase of a bike odometer.

I could have simply driven around my neighborhood, measuring out that one kilometer with my car's odometer, but I felt the need to have my wife share in the pain I was about to put myself through. More truthfully, and since it would at most be 1KM, I figured that by installing an odometer on her bike I would be more inclined to push myself further with her there beside me. Or perhaps and to be even more honest, I felt that I wouldn't give up as quickly if she were there beside me, nagging me about why I'd want to have a heart attack out in the street.

Yes, she had to suffer alongside me.

13

I pulled my vehicle up the driveway and into the garage, hoping she wouldn't hear the garage door rattling up. I wanted to install the odometer on her bike without her catching me in the act. I wanted to surprise her but not necessarily in a good way. It was more like I assumed she'd try to stop me had she seen me. She hated biking, even though I'm sure the bikes were her idea, as I hated biking even more.

I'd managed to only find some tools in my 'I have no idea what I'm doing with tools' toolbox when my wife came out, wondering what I was up to. I was more or less caught in the act so I decided that I might as well share my surprise.

"I'm putting an odometer on your bike," I started, wondering how she'd take that. "I figured you could ride beside me while I went on my run today, to see how far I can go."

"You really thought you needed an odometer to run three blocks?" A playful smile ran across her lips once more.

14

Everyone finds inspiration in different places. The inspiration I needed that day was in her sarcasm. I desperately wanted to prove to myself that I could run farther - a lot farther - but I also wanted her to eat her words. That, honestly, was the real motivation. One kilometer was no longer my goal. I wasn't sure what my new goal would be, but I knew that one kilometer wouldn't be sufficient.

15

After a couple more hours of swearing, stripping bolts and making a mental note to upgrade my Fisher Price toolbox, the odometer was installed.

Getting her out the door had taken more convincing than I would have thought, but in the end, using her own sarcasm against her seemed to do the trick. Could she not handle a three-block bike ride to support her husband's weight-loss plan?

16

We headed out together, my wife now trying to be supportive but also concerned about the darkening skies. She didn't like getting wet and it definitely looked like rain was imminent.

We passed the two houses on the way to the end of our street, turned right and then followed the same route I'd run the previous two days. I held my slow, jogging pace despite the fact that my wife could barely keep the bike upright going that slow.

We passed the first electrical box, then the second. My heart was definitely banging around in my chest, so I took some long, deep breaths and focused on maintaining my slow but steady pace.

We crossed the next street leading into another cul-de-sac, then the next. I was already at four blocks and was proud of my accomplishment but was nowhere near ready to turn around. Instead, we turned onto a bike path and cut out of our subdivision towards the neighboring farmer's field.

"You've got to be kidding," she said, realizing that the gravel road onto which we'd turned was at least one kilometer in length, possibly more.

"Don't worry, you know I won't make it more than a couple hundred meters before I have to turn around." The words came out of my mouth, but I didn't believe them. I'd said them only to keep her at my side, measuring this run.

"Stephen, those clouds aren't a joke. We'll get soaked!" she protested.

"Last I checked you weren't made of sugar. And I don't think you're a witch..." I winked at her. "Suck it up, support me!"

To her credit, she did. I didn't hear another complaint out of her, not even when the rain started coming down in sheets.

17

I had run the entire length of the farmer's field - which I had assumed was 1KM - and approached an intersection marking the first corner. The skies definitely looked ominous though the rain hadn't started in yet.

Instead of turning around and heading back, I rounded the corner of the field and headed to my left, starting down that seemingly endless road. My wife turned the corner beside me and continued without complaint.

I ran and I ran, all the while focusing on two things: keeping my heart rate in check by maintaining a slow and easy pace, and my breathing.

A few times she wanted to tell me how far I'd run but I made it very clear that I had no interest in knowing until we were back at home. I no longer cared about hitting a specific distance; instead, it was about running until I couldn't run any more. I had already surpassed the first goal of four blocks that I had set for the day, then my dream goal of one kilometer, or so I had hoped. Then I had started realizing that goals were just limits as well: limits of my confidence.

18

We came to the next corner of that farmer's field, the farthest point from our house on that run. I was tired and sore and I could definitely feel my right foot and leg giving me grief. It felt like I was running on a fractured ankle while my right leg throbbed with the beat of my heart. However, I wasn't about to let them make me stop. I had experienced hard days at work where my ankle and foot swelled up substantially and hurt incredibly. I was accustomed to pain so all that mattered was moving forward until I absolutely had to stop, and I didn't think that was going to happen any time soon.

I'd decided that I was going to run around the entire farmer's field and I wasn't going to deviate from that plan. My wife had started out as the motivation, but I'd found new motivation within myself. That motivation was something new to me: I was finally proud of myself.

19

The rain started coming down, just a sprinkle at first. I was grateful for it as I was starting to mist up and I didn't want my wife to see.

I'd had such poor self-esteem for so long and I honestly never thought I was capable of doing something like that run. I'd lost my confidence despite the fact that I was an important person for a very large company, despite the fact that I had wealth and a 'perfect' life in the eyes of so many. Yet none of that meant anything to me; that run seemed to mean the world. I fought back the tears and pushed on.

A few moments later the drizzle turned to large drops. Then, just when we thought we couldn't get any wetter, the skies opened up and it poured.

I went from sniveling to laughing and my wife joined in. There was no point in complaining; we were a long way from home and there was no shelter out here. However, even if there was, I wouldn't have taken it.

The gravel road quickly became slick. My t-shirt and shorts clung to me, making me feel desperately cold despite the heat I was generating from running.

I knew that if I was cold, my wife would have been freezing, especially considering that she weighed about half of what I weighed, and she wasn't wearing anything warm.

I glanced over at her and noticed her quivering blue lips. She was, in fact, freezing but still hadn't complained. She would tell me later that she felt there was no way she could give up on me when I wasn't giving up on myself, especially considering all that I'd gone through. She liked to tease and taunt me, like any good wife I suppose, but deep down she knew I had my demons to battle and that I was trying to make a positive change. Although we were in a bad state by then and our marriage didn't last, it's a moment I will always cherish, just like our friendship, which has lasted even to today.

20

It was hard seeing her suffer like that and especially at my hand. I suggested that she should either bike quickly back to our house or ride ahead, then double back for me, then repeat. This way, she could bike faster and warm up but she wouldn't have it. Biking like that meant adding extra distance that I wouldn't be running, and she wanted the distance to come out correctly on the odometer. I then suggested that we drive it afterwards to check the distance. However, she stuck there beside me, occasionally checking in to see how I was doing. Other than that, she left me to focus on my run.

21

I rounded the third corner of the farmer's field while the rain continued to pound us. Despite feeling like I was freezing and the pain in my leg and foot, I was also feeling ecstatic!

I felt at peace and it brought me a new energy that surged through my body. I was proud of myself, and this made me want to push myself even more, to run faster. However, I resisted the urge to speed up, knowing that I had already been at my limit for some time.

22

I pushed onwards, focusing on the next corner of the field, which seemed way too far away. I wiped the sweat and rain from my forehead and eyes, then started drifting off with my thoughts.

A moment or two later my wife noticed my right foot. She had been keeping a close eye on me, watching for signs of a heart attack perhaps, but also just watching over me in general. She still cared, and it touched me.

"Your foot!" she said. "I think you're bleeding!"

I looked down and noticed that blood was seeping out the front of my right sneaker every time I landed on that foot. Most of the toe box was red despite the rain.

"Wow," I said. "That would explain some of what I'm feeling in my foot!"

My foot had started bothering me shortly after I'd started the run, but I had simply assumed it was due to my general foot issues – nothing more. However, after all the years of surgeries and everything else, my foot had never bled, at least not that I could recall.

"Well, there's not much I can do about that now," I said matter-of-factly. I pressed on and tried to ignore what I'd seen.

23

We rounded the final corner of the farmer's field and headed back towards our subdivision. The rain was letting up and we were both beaming. Again, my wife had wanted to share with me how far I had run but I didn't want to know until we reached our driveway. By my calculation, we had only another 300 or 400 meters to go.

Three hundred or four hundred meters to go! I thought. I realized that in the past 15 years, excluding the current run, I had run only a total of 300 meters, and all in the past 48 hours. Now that would be my final stretch of this run. I was beside myself and somewhat in disbelief!

I really wanted to sprint the last few hundred meters but held steady. Besides, I wasn't sure if my legs, heart or bleeding foot could handle it, even at the very end of the run.

We turned onto our street together, my wife still by my side. We were then about 50 meters from our driveway which marked my finish line – or so I'd thought.

"Don't stop at the driveway, keep going!" she said, a wild grin spreading across her face.

"You're kidding me, right?" I said, flabbergasted. "There's no way I'm going on. I crushed all my expectations but now I'm ready for a hot shower. Then I'm going to die on the sofa, if that's OK with you!"

"No, you're going to need to trust me. Keep running, just a little more. Maybe one more block. Please, you won't regret it!"

I wasn't sure how I could say no when she'd stuck by me all that time in the pouring rain, freezing and not complaining. Besides, she wouldn't have pressured me into running farther unless it really mattered.

I assumed we were coming up on a round number of kilometers. By my best guess, which is never something to bet on, I assumed that to be five kilometers. If I was right, I was definitely going to celebrate!

"Ugh." I sighed. "OK, let's do this!"

We passed our driveway and I continued my hobble of a run to the end of our block, around the corner and onto the street behind our house. I saw the first electrical box there, no longer mocking me. I ran towards it, limping profoundly but grinning like a shark sneaking up on his unsuspecting lunch.

I had plans to kick that electrical box when I reached it, then thought better of it considering my bloody foot. Instead, I thought, *I'll give it a slap while running past*. It would have to do.

I was lost in thought again, trying to avoid thinking about running, the pain or getting home when my wife bellowed at me: "STOP!"

"Whaaa?" I mumbled. "What the..."

But she cut me off.

"Stephen! Stop! Here!"

And so I stopped, less than a few feet from that metal electrical box and only 100 meters or so from my front door.

24

I was grateful to stop, absolutely delighted to stop, but also wanted to make it to that metal, mocking beast and slap it. Hard.

My foot was throbbing, my leg ached and now I just wanted to be home. Although it was only a two-minute walk away, it felt like a thousand miles now that I'd finally stopped running.

Keep walking. I thought. *Just keep walking.*

I hobbled towards that electrical box, now wanting only to sit on it again.

After finally catching my breath, I asked: "What gives?" Emotions were sneaking up on me again and I was trying to contain them.

She tapped the odometer a few times as if to ensure that it wasn't lying to her. I let her do her thing while I closed in on that metal box.

"I can't believe it!" she finally said. She tapped it some more.

"What? I'm dying here! Physically and emotionally. What can't you believe?"

"Ten kilometers!" she said. "You just ran exactly 10 kilometers! I'm so proud of you!"

I couldn't believe it. Ten kilometers! From 100 meters two days ago and feeling like I was going to die, to running 200 meters the day before and feeling the same, to running 10 kilometers without stopping! There was no containing the emotions as they poured over me. My wife rode up beside me and hugged me tightly, telling me how proud she was.

I was in total shock and disbelief. Not in my wildest dreams would I have thought it possible. I took a moment and a deep breath.

It was a beautiful moment for many reasons, some of them obvious, but it was also when I realized that I had to learn to prevent my personal beliefs from ever limiting me again.

I knew I'd have to work on it and I vowed that I would. From that day forward, I started by recognizing when I was making excuses about what I could and couldn't do. Then I changed my terminology from 'can't' to 'can', thus freeing myself from those tricky limitations.

25

My wife was going on and on about being proud of me and I was trying to soak it up while not thinking about the pain coursing through my body. It was bittersweet. I don't think my wife had ever once told me that she was proud of me – and honestly, I don't think I had ever felt so proud of myself.

We made it back to our house and I opened the garage door. I wanted to make a beeline for the bathtub, but she wanted to check out my foot first.

I took off my shoe and noted my sock, blood-soaked from the toes to about midfoot. I was more than a little concerned about the cause of the blood, thinking that maybe running wasn't such a good thing for me after all. If that was the case, I would be devastated.

I hesitantly peeled off the sock. To my horror, I noticed a huge flap of skin hanging between two of my toes. I was confused at first, then started chuckling with relief. My concerns about not being able to run again were unfounded and I learned another lesson about running: short toenails are critical!

Because my right foot is shaped like a large, reversed letter C, it curves substantially, cramping the toes together. My smallest toenail had cut a trench into the next toe over, causing the blood and pain.

I washed off with the garden hose, making a mental note to trim my toenails before my next run.

My next run? I thought. Despite the pain, I was already thinking about the next and I couldn't have been happier.

Chapter 7 – An Addict Is Born

I had discovered two major keys to running longer distances during my 10-kilometer run: pace and breathing. I figured that if I maintained a pace that my heart and lungs could keep up with, I'd keep my breathing in check and I would be able to run for much longer distances. The only thing I wasn't sure about was how to manage the pain in my foot and leg. However, I assumed that with time and consistent training, both would strengthen and that those issues would resolve themselves. Or at least, that was the hope.

2

I spent the first week after that 10-kilometer run recovering from what I'd put my body through. I avoided being on the sales floor at work due to being sore from basically the hips down. My ankle and foot were severely swollen and ached something fierce. I had really punished my body during that run as I hadn't previously done any exercise … well … pretty much ever.

However, even though I wasn't running that week, I was planning all sorts of runs in my head. I'd been fired up after my first 100-meter run, but I was absolutely hooked after the 10-

kilometer run and decided that this was going to be how I improved my health. There would be no easing into it, clearly, as going from two blocks to 10 kilometers isn't exactly easing into anything. I was fully committed.

I created a basic running routine that included a five-kilometer loop around my neighborhood, six days a week. Then, each Sunday, I would test myself both physically and mentally by running as far as I could in one direction. Once I reached my limit, I would call the wife and ask her to come and get me, allowing me to focus simply on running as far as I possibly could.

I was unbelievably excited to start my routine in general but more excited to try running in one direction to see if I could best my 10-kilometer run, as difficult as I thought that would be. However, I forced myself to wait until the following Sunday, allowing my battered body to recover as much as possible.

3

When the next Sunday morning finally arrived, I had quickly hopped out of bed and into my gear, eager to get at the run. I had surprised myself with this new-found desire to do something healthy and to start my day so early when any previous Sunday morning typically didn't start until around midday.

My leg and foot still ached and were swollen, but the pain wasn't severe enough to stop me from heading out the front door. Nothing, in fact, was going to stop me from heading out the door.

Looking back, I really don't know where I found the energy to get out and run. My work schedule was incredible and my stress levels were through the roof. Sunday was my only free day and even then, I had spent a third of the day on the phone and another third of the day at one of my many store locations, trying to straighten out one problem or another. Yet clearly my desire for positive change trumped everything else. I found that running had given me more energy rather than take it away.

4

We lived on the very southwest edge of the city in a brand-new neighborhood which meant newly paved roads, long stretches of tree- and shrub-lined sidewalk and very few people, especially at that hour of the day. I felt like I had the entire neighborhood to myself.

I somehow had an abundance of energy and had to remind myself about not going out too fast. I had to focus on distance, not speed. That would come with time as I lost weight and put on muscle mass. However, patience had never been my strong suit. I had remembered something I had read about how when we spend years abusing our bodies, we can't expect them to rebound in days. Months, perhaps, but not days. I tried to keep that in mind and headed out the door while my wife continued to sleep.

5

I started out that day by running the first half of my neighborhood five-kilometer loop. However, rather than continuing to follow the main road that would eventually circle back to my house, I turned onto the street that connected my neighborhood to running parts unknown. It was exciting to exit my neighborhood under my own steam and I soaked up the feeling of doing something beneficial for my body rather than abusing it like I was accustomed to doing at the time.

6

The run started out well despite a throbbing right foot that I tried hard to ignore. I remembered again that I could have been at work experiencing the same pain, so I considered myself very fortunate and pressed on.

Once I determined that I was roughly five kilometers into my run, I went through a few checks in my mind: breathing (heavy but consistent), heart (beating fast but not too fast), left leg (a little sore but warming up to the run), right leg and foot (quite painful but manageable).

Although I didn't want to limit my run by setting a goal distance, I did want to have a minimum distance goal to push myself. I didn't think that running 10 kilometers again would be an issue, but I wondered if I could somehow manage 15 kilometers. I certainly wanted to best my last long run but also didn't want to overdo it or set myself up for disappointment. Besides, aiming for something more reasonable like 11 kilometers would have made sense. Small steps, I thought that would be the smart thing to do. Then again, I could only guess as to how far I was running as I hadn't previously marked out my route. And, if GPS watches even existed back then, I wouldn't have known what one was.

I decided that there was only one thing to do: run as far as I could in one direction, as per my original plan.

7

As any runner knows, there's something pretty special about running in the early morning, before the traffic starts and the sun gets too hot. It's like our special alone time to reflect and maybe sort out problems, or just zone out and enjoy the moment.

However, if one doesn't zone out, a lot runs through the mind when running distance. We start to remember all the things we forgot that day, the previous day and most of the past month as well. We make grocery lists, have conversations in our heads with our bosses (and say things we would never dare say to them in person), and occasionally solve the world's biggest problems.

We zone out, we zone in, we babble to ourselves, catch ourselves doing it, look around embarrassed, then do it again unknowingly.

We pretend we're on a tropical vacation. We dream about quitting our jobs and moving to Europe or an island ... this, that or the other thing. However, most of all, we fantasize about eating. Join any running group anywhere in the world and within a few minutes, all conversations turn to food – our favorite foods, what we ate for breakfast, what we should have eaten for breakfast, what we're going to eat after the run and, of course, all the foods and beverages that will clog your arteries and damage your liver, but that would be good in that moment.

The farther we run the further we take things in our minds and conversations. And for some, on really long runs, the mind starts playing tricks. We can go for a ride on an emotional rollercoaster. We get that runner's high, we hit some low points, we pretend we're actually on a racecourse with people cheering us on and of course, religious or not, we pray. We pray for the run to be over; we pray that we don't become injured, and we pray that there's going to be a fat piece of cheesecake, a big juicy steak or an ice-cold beer waiting for us at the finish line. Or all three.

Of course, all these things happen more to newbies than to seasoned runners. That's because of one main thing: lack of calories.

Many people who get into running do so to lose weight. However, they decide to ramp up the exercise routine while dieting at the same time. It's a terrible combination that leads to both injury and the ridiculousness that runs through our heads.

On that second long run I started falling victim to the ups and downs, the emotions and crazy thoughts multiplied by all the stress and turbulence in my life at the time. Unfortunately, I had no idea what was happening to me, but I thought that maybe I was going crazy.

I laughed, I was somber, I sniveled and I cried. Then I did it all over again and had no idea why I felt like I was going through puberty again, experiencing the entire range of emotions within a span of 10 minutes.

A few weeks before I got into running, the wife and I had started a highly restrictive crash diet. I was all but starving myself. Then, when I started running, instead of upping my caloric intake, I reduced it further. I was basically operating on fumes on a regular basis – and worse, doing so when I was running. It was a terrible combination and it was beating me up on that run. Instead of connecting the dots, I simply thought that I was going a little crazy.

8

I had run from my far, southwest corner of the city all the way to downtown, crossed the river that snaked its way through the center of the city, and was now running towards the northeast. I thought I had run roughly 8 kilometers but was afraid it may have been less.

What I *was* sure about was that I was a hot, sloppy mess, beyond tired, starving and ready to call it quits. However, how could I stop if I thought it was around 8 kilometers? For some crazy reason, I felt that if I couldn't best my previous 10 kilometers then I wasn't progressing, even though I had run it only one week previously.

I ran through another body check and was happy to realize that my heart, lungs and left leg were all doing well. Some strange aches and pains had come and gone, but I had run through them all. My only real concern was my right leg and foot, both of which were throbbing and in real pain. My limp was much more pronounced, and I felt like I was hobbling more than running, but still I pushed on. I had to push on.

9

The sun had risen substantially since I'd started the run and I felt extremely hot and thirsty. I hadn't thought to bring a bottle of water. Another rookie move. Not having water on my 10 kilometers hadn't been an issue as that day had been so much cooler, especially with the rain. However, this day was brutally hot.

Worse, the emotional rollercoaster was back and I was in the front seat, experiencing every rise and fall. I started making some major realizations – or, rather, the run made me start to own up to them – about my life, my health, my relationship with my wife and my career. Running was now in my life, but it was time to look at fixing the other issues.

Thinking about all my unresolved issues seemed to drain me further. I realized that I was going to have to stop my run sooner rather than later. I was all but spent.

10

I had brought a couple of coins to call either an ambulance or my wife, depending on how the run went. Although I probably would have been put on fluids had I called the ambulance, I decided that I'd be calling the wife instead.

Back then, phone booths were still very common, so I simply had to choose one and call. That call, of course, meant that I'd given up on the run. For some reason, I felt that it meant that I was giving up on myself. By then I was fairly certain that I hadn't run more than 10 kilometers although there was no way I could know for sure.

11

Being very overweight and realizing that it's your own fault can play some real tricks on your emotions. Back then, I constantly beat myself up about being overweight. Honestly, even today, I still have a few lingering body image issues that I'll eventually get around to fixing. Eventually. However, on that particular run, I felt like I had to punish myself for my previous lack of self-control.

So, despite feeling like hell and with my body breaking down and my mind making me think crazy thoughts, I ran past a bank of phone booths. I pushed on.

12

To keep going, I set bite-sized goals. *Just make it to the next streetlamp,* I would think. Then, once I made it there, *just make it to the next street corner.* Once I made it to the next streetlamp or corner, I'd find the next marker and push myself to that.

I repeated this process, streetlamp to streetlamp, corner to corner, focusing solely on the next marker.

I hadn't stopped running since I'd left my front door, but I knew that was going to change shortly. Yet, I somehow managed another two minutes of running, then another five minutes, then another hour. I was shocked that I was still able to push myself, despite being physically drained and in immense pain and without having had a drop of water or a bite of food.

I had run straight across the city when I finally allowed myself to stop.

I had run myself to the point of exhaustion. I was more than a little wobbly but very pleased with my performance, especially that last push. I had run until I thought I couldn't run any farther, then pushed myself to the next limit, broke through that wall and then even farther. I had nothing left to prove that day. I was done.

Although I wanted to best the previous Sunday, I had decided that I had to be happy with whatever distance I covered because I couldn't have made it another 10 feet. Besides, my right foot and ankle had swollen to the point that I was certain I'd have to cut off my shoe and sock.

13

I made the phone call from a dirty phone booth, leaning against its wall for support as I could barely stand. My wife answered on the first ring, her voice shaking. I had been out running so long she'd been worried that I may have actually had a heart attack.

I apologized for scaring her and told her where I was. She quickly agreed to come get me after making some joke about my maybe wanting to run back.

We shared a laugh over her comment. There was no way I could run another 100 meters if my life depended on it. I had left absolutely 100 percent of myself out there and the tank had nothing left. Nothing. Besting that run would take nothing short of a miracle. That I knew.

14

During my run, I'd made sure to follow the most direct route possible so that we could return home the same way afterwards, measuring the distance. Therefore, when my wife finally pulled up to our meeting point, she already knew how far I had run and was eager to tell me. I, on the other hand, had no interest in hearing unless I was absolutely certain she hadn't taken any detours.

I had her reset the trip odometer and we drove back home, mostly in silence, as I kept nodding off, barely able to keep myself from falling into a deep, food-deprived and exercise-induced coma. When I was coherent, I remember hoping that I really had run 11 kilometers, or at least close to it. I felt I deserved it considering what I'd put myself through. However, I also didn't want to get my hopes up so I kept reminding myself that it was only the fourth run of my life and that I was just starting; improvement would come over time. Besides, I thought, I had to factor in my foot and leg and just be grateful that I could run at all.

When we finally turned into our driveway, my wife shook me awake and pointed at the odometer. I was certain that I was still delirious, as Trip A read just over 18 kilometers.

Chapter 8 – The New York City Marathon

I gave myself most of the following week off, partly as a reward for beating the 15-kilometer dream goal that I'd secretly set for myself but mostly because I could barely walk. My right leg was giving me a lot of grief and my right foot and ankle were dangerously swollen. On top of that and due to my extremely poor biomechanics, my hips and back were very sore which made basically everything either a struggle or painful.

Putting on my work shoes the next day meant that a substantial amount of water-filled skin was flopping over the top edge of my shoe. That foot had next to no circulation. It was brutal but the feeling of accomplishment far outweighed the pain.

When I did start running again, and after my foot and ankle had returned to as normal-looking as they get, I followed my plan by running the five-kilometer loop around my neighborhood six days a week before work. I reserved Sundays for trying to outdo my previous Sunday long run. I realized that I was going to experience pain; that was not completely avoidable. However, I made an appointment with a podiatrist to see if they had suggestions on how I could lessen it.

My 5K weekday runs quickly became fairly easy when I remembered my pace and breathing. Eventually I found myself wanting to run two loops around the neighborhood. However, most days I held myself back and kept the main prize in mind: my Sunday long run.

I'd quickly become hooked on running despite the fact that I hadn't run my entire life. However, having found running, I now felt that I couldn't live without it. It was my drug of choice, my mistress, and we weren't to be separated. Even after seeing the podiatrist and being told that I was only going to create additional issues by continuing to run, I walked out of the office with no intent of stopping. I felt that I knew my body better than they did and that if it truly became a serious issue, I would stop – but then and only then. Until that day came, if it ever did, I would continue running.

Weeks went by and I continued to run my routine. My Sunday long runs didn't always best the previous ones in distance, but I certainly bested them in time. I was leaning out quickly and becoming considerably faster. I started reading about proper hydration, clothing and running shoes. I even read about proper nutrition but that I mostly ignored.

Regardless of my ignorance, in just over four and a half months I had dropped 75 pounds.

2

Around the same time I started running, a childhood friend also began running to lose weight. Although we never trained together, as he had focused on speed whereas I had focused on distance, we did manage to get in a few fun runs together, and then a 22-kilometer race.

We enjoyed racing together, supporting each other even though he always beat me. I would have been happy to continue like that, running my own schedule, focusing on beating my previous personal bests, getting in local races, but Clinton always had a way of thinking big.

One evening in the spring of 2000 he called me up and asked if I was interested in running the New York City Marathon.

Although I'd been running for just over four months and had a couple of races under my belt, I was far from educated in the sport. I made that far-too-common mistake of assuming that all races were called "marathons." So rather than ask Clinton how far this particular marathon was and because I had never been to New York, I simply told him that I was absolutely interested and to sign me up.

I gave Clinton my credit card number and let him take care of the details. I trusted him and didn't bother to ask any questions about the race. Besides, what was there to ask? It was running and it was in New York!

3

I was considerably slimmer and faster by that point and no longer running just to lose weight. I was thinking about longer distances and faster times, constantly trying to outdo my previous bests. I wanted to do the same in New York. However, to do that, I needed some information from Clinton – mainly how long this particular marathon was going to be.

"It's a *marathon*!" he said when he finally stopped laughing.

"Yes, I'm aware of that," I said, bewildered. "But how long is it?"

"Um, marathon distance. To be precise, 42.195 kilometers."

Although I can't be certain, I believe I may have stopped breathing.

"Are you kidding me?" I finally managed. "Is that even possible?"

"Yes, I assure you it is. However, whether *we* can run that far remains to be seen."

I was shocked and terrified. What had I gotten myself into? I leaned back in my chair and pondered what he had just told me.

4

I put down the phone, shaking. What had I done? I'd signed myself up for a race without knowing the distance and it was almost double my longest race to date! Was I crazy? Was Clinton crazy for suggesting it? Was it too late to cancel?

It scared me half to death but at the same time another feeling started to wash over me: excitement.

On more than one occasion I've had this strange mixture of feeling sick to my stomach about taking on a race, then having it slowly turn to excitement. It's an initial 'there's no way I can do it' feeling that slowly turns into 'well, I guess there's a possibility' which then turns into 'maybe I can do it' and then, finally, 'of course I can!'

Slowly, the feeling of fear dissipated and the feeling of excitement took over. I decided that it was just another challenge and I was certainly up for it. The only thing I really had to do was find a real training plan.

5

I had remembered seeing a group of runners in my neighborhood some Sunday mornings. When I first saw them, I typically watched them go by while I sat on my sofa, watching a movie and trying to eat my way through a family-sized bag of chips. Then, after I started running, I had occasionally come across them while out running and without potato chip dust on my shirt.

I started thinking about this group now that I was running and had accidentally signed up for a marathon.

After doing a little research I found out that the group was with The Running Room and they offered running classes. I quickly signed up for their marathon training program.

Honestly, by then I was more intimidated about joining a group of runners than I was about running the marathon. However, I also wanted to do well in New York and not simply cross the finish line. Or worse – not cross it.

After the first few minutes on the very first day, I realized there nothing to be intimidated by. Everyone seemed to be just different versions of myself: there to lose weight, tackle a new goal or maintain their physical health. No one was there to show off or belittle us beginners. I instantly felt like I was part of something bigger than myself and I was grateful for both The Running Room and its program.

6

My training went well and I found myself looking forward to the weekly class and group runs. I felt that I had a new family, and we were all improving together as a team, despite my previously thinking that running was an individual sport.

I was learning a lot about running and in an enjoyable way. I had no idea there was so much to know about a sport that was seemingly about 'one foot in front of the other.' That couldn't have been further from the truth.

As I started my official training, I also continued to slim down, but I was no longer just losing fat; I was also putting on muscle mass. For the first time in my life, I started feeling good about my body. My clothes started hanging properly rather than clinging to me uncomfortably. My inner thighs stopped rubbing together when I walked or ran and I stopped trying to hide my body under unnecessary layers of clothing.

To be honest, the experience was overwhelming as a large part of me had assumed that I would always be overweight, that I would never have proper self-control over my eating and exercise. Of course, none of that was true. The reality was that my previously obese body and my failing health were my own fault and that I most certainly had self-control, I just hadn't exercised that control previously. I had to accept that I'd been making excuses and then worse, believing those excuses and allowing them to dictate my life.

I had to own up to that fact. However, rather than simply beat myself up about the past, which I really had been doing all my life, I started to realize that I was doing something about it and making a positive change. Of that I was extremely proud and decided to focus my attention there instead.

7

The 18-week-long Running Room course flew by and before I knew it, I was ready to head to New York.

My right foot and ankle had given me plenty of grief over those weeks and they basically stayed swollen the entire time. However, I also noticed that they seemed to strengthen as well. They must have as when the weekly training mileage increased, I didn't feel any worse for the wear. Even running the 29K and 32K Sunday long runs near the end of the training schedule, they seemed to feel the same as back when I was running the 5K loops around my neighborhood.

I also noticed something amazing: my right foot didn't seem to have such an extreme curve to it as it had before I started running. Rather than curving inwards as much as it had, it appeared a little straighter. Not much, but enough to notice and it certainly felt better in my running shoes.

8

Although Clinton and I had trained separately, we agreed to start the marathon together then let whatever happened on the course happen. I certainly didn't want to hold him back from running his own race as I figured he would be much faster.

If you've never run the New York City Marathon you're missing out on perhaps the greatest marathon on the planet. Lining up on the Verrazano-Narrows Bridge with tens of thousands of other runners is an experience that one never forgets! Standing shoulder-to-shoulder with runners from all over the world who have come to New York to run the five boroughs together is an experience all runners must have at least once in their lives. The brotherly and sisterly love and unity of people who can't even speak the same language, who have different ethnic backgrounds, beliefs or religions, statuses and body types is truly amazing. It doesn't matter who you are or where you're from, what you do for a living, whether this is your first or 100th marathon, or whether you're 18 or 81, you are part of one big family.

People were hugging and cheering as if we were all long-lost friends and had just finished the race together ... and it hadn't even begun! People were doing the wave, high-fiving and rallying. People on both sides of me grabbed me and said hello, asked me where I was from and then hugged me as if we had known each other for years. I was blown away, shocked and in love all at the same time.

The energy was something I had never experienced before. To this day, I still get tingles when I think about it.

Then, in the middle of this amazing moment, the loudspeakers started booming out Frank Sinatra's "New York, New York" and everyone joined in, held hands, embraced and swayed in time. I was lost in a wave of people and emotions.

In that phenomenal moment I started remembering how I'd gotten there and where

I'd come from. I started remembering the changes my body had gone through and my previous attitude towards my body in general. I remembered dealing with the surgeries, doctors' visits, crutches and pain. Then something else happened: I felt proud. Proud of myself for all I'd endured to get to that starting line and for pushing through the incredibly tough times. It wasn't a feeling I was accustomed to and I felt my throat hitch and my body tremble.

A little embarrassed, I wiped away a few tears only to notice that I wasn't alone. Far from it, in fact. I made out one of those awkward laugh-cries sounds, held back more tears and shifted my feet.

9

BOOM! BOOM! Two cannons fired at the end of the song, signaling the start of the race. Close to 40,000 runners started moving forward as one, shuffling at first due to the extreme congestion, then walking briskly, then running. It was finally happening; I was going to run a marathon! I *was* running a marathon! Against all odds, the kid who had constantly been reminded of his limitations and inability to run was about to start what was arguably the greatest marathon on the planet. I could hardly believe it!

We started running up and over the Verrazano-Narrows Bridge, a double-decker bridge that was full of runners both up and down the entire length of its 4 plus kilometer span. Clinton and I tried to hold a slower pace off the start, but it was hard with all the adrenaline pumping through our veins. I expected to beat four hours but at the pace we were running, had I maintained it, I would have finished in less than three hours. That excited me but it was also a rookie move. There wasn't even a slight possibility that I could run a marathon that much faster than what I had trained for. However, I *was* a rookie and so once we reached the highest point on the bridge and then headed down the backside, rather than slowing down or maintaining pace, we sped up.

10

We ran together, finally settling into a more reasonable pace and one that was considerably slower than the one at which we'd started. We were back on for a four-hour finish and we held that same pace until about the 30-kilometer mark without much issue.

My right leg and foot were complaining plenty, of course, but I numbed them with a considerable and unhealthy number of painkillers. I wasn't about to let pain take this race away from me. I swore that I would finish it by crawling if I had to.

Clinton, having grown up with me, knew my situation and checked in with me a few times. I always gave him the nod that everything was good. There was no point in complaining about something I couldn't change.

Instead, I plodded on, growing a bit tired and weary as we neared the three-hour mark.

11

In training I'd run up to 32 kilometers so I was now closing in on new territory. It was exciting, as every step I took meant a new personal best in distance. At the same time, my body was starting to break down. The idea of running 'only' 10 more kilometers was daunting, to say the least.

I tried not to think about the distance. Instead, I focused on what I was doing. Clinton tried to make small talk with me but that was no longer working. I was desperately tired and now starving as I'd brought only a sports drink and no food. *'Only' 10 more kilometers*, my mind screamed. *'Only…'*

I knew that I was holding Clinton back but somehow during his training he had managed to sneak in the Rome Marathon, so he wasn't concerned about time. Rather, he just wanted to run together and share the experience. I was grateful even if I no longer wanted to talk to him or hear him talk to me.

I had to get through the last 10 kilometers, so I started focusing on what I'd gone through to get to this place, the hard work, the dedication and all my long runs. I realized that 10 kilometers equaled two loops around my neighborhood, something I'd run a hundred times and with relative ease. I just had to do that distance one last time and then never, ever again. I'd decided this was a 'one-and-done' type of scenario. As much as I loved to run, I wouldn't ever tackle such a distance again. Never. Ever.

12

We had run through four boroughs of New York and were now entering Manhattan. The crowds of people watching and cheering us on had been a real shock to me. I saw more people lining the course than I'd seen in my entire life. I remember watching the news afterwards which had estimated that more than three million people had turned out to line the streets. I had no idea what that many people looked like, but I recall that some parts of the sidewalk lining the course were five and six people deep for as far as the eye could see.

As we ran alongside Central Park and towards Columbus Circle, where the course would turn into the park, the crowds were deafening. It surprised me to still see such an incredible number of people after almost four hours as I assumed they really only wanted to see the front runners. However, that was far from the case.

Before starting the marathon, Clinton had suggested that I write my name across the chest of my shirt as New Yorkers would personalize my race by calling out my name. He wasn't wrong and I constantly heard people cheering me on. It was amazing and always gave me an additional jolt of energy. In between people calling out my name, children held out pieces of bananas, oranges and candy which I happily took while high-fiving others.

More people held out napkins to wipe our faces and sponges to cool our necks and heads. All throughout the course we read hilarious, inspiring and hopeful signs. Not only did New Yorkers accept the fact that a bunch of crazy runners had crippled their city's traffic for the day, but they were also legitimately enjoying the spectacle of watching around 40,000 runners pound the streets to collect a finisher's medal and t-shirt. It seemed surreal!

13

We'd run so far and yet it seemed we still had forever to go. We were now down to the final five kilometers, the equivalent of one lap around my neighborhood – the shortest run of my week. That's all I had left, but it still seemed like forever.

I'd started out with so much energy and confidence but by then the gas tank was empty and I was running on sheer determination. Plus, my goal of finishing in four hours or less was quickly falling away.

I'd convinced Clinton to run ahead as I'd started slowing down somewhere around the 35-kilometer mark. I knew Clinton hadn't been concerned about time, but I didn't want to slow him down too much. Despite the fistful of pills I'd consumed, my right leg and foot were getting the better of me.

It wasn't that I didn't want Clinton to run with me. However, I could feel myself becoming more discouraged when I was forced to slow down – and, of course, by the pain.

I started to consider that perhaps I wasn't meant to run after all. Or at least not these sorts of distances.

Instead of entertaining more thoughts like that, I tried to run a little taller, put my chin up and push myself harder. Only one more loop around the neighborhood, then this craziness would end!

14

That surge lasted only so long before I decided that I needed a break. My body felt like it was breaking down, I was completely out of energy and now my right ankle was killing me. I felt like I was going to need an entirely new right leg after the race.

I was in Central Park and pulling off to the side of the course, slowing right down from my slow hobble of a run to a slower hobble of a walk.

"Hey, Steve, did you come to New York to walk or run?" I heard someone yelling in my direction. Were they talking to me, I thought? Impossible, but then we made eye contact.

It took me a moment to realize that, no, I didn't know him, yet he spoke again.

"Yeah, I'm talking to you, Steve. Get your butt moving! Seriously, you didn't come to New York to walk the marathon! You can do it, buddy!"

In the span of only the past few kilometers I'd been so lost in thought that I'd forgotten that I'd written my name on my shirt.

"Come on, Steve!" chirped someone else. "You can do this! Only three miles to go! You got this!"

Then more people called out to me, sensing my desperation and need for help in that moment. Complete strangers worked together to give me a much-needed push. It was absolutely incredible and it was impossible to not feel moved.

They continued calling out to me and cheering me on until I went from my hobble of a walk back to my hobble of a run, slow at first, then speeding up with their cheers. I felt like a superstar!

15

The people of New York may never know how important they are to us runners while we invade their city, but they are absolutely vital! Any runner who has ever run the New York City Marathon will say the same. That's what makes this particular marathon so amazing! Of course, running in New York is amazing in general, through all the boroughs and with all those people. However, the magic lies in those special New Yorkers, lining the streets in droves during the marathon, cheering us on with their inspirational signs and chants from start to finish.

16

I was down to the final kilometer and the pain and overwhelming desire for this craziness to stop started to dissipate. The crowds seemed even larger, the screams even louder. My energy was restored with every high-five and every shout of my name.

I managed my old pace again, maybe even a little quicker. Then I saw Clinton up just ahead of me in the maze of people. My childhood friend, whom I'd met when I was only five, had slowed down to allow me to catch up so that we could not only start this race together, but finish it together as well.

He patted me on the back, grabbed my hand and held it up high in victory as we ran to the cheers of thousands of spectators and flashing cameras.

We crossed the finish line a few seconds later and I couldn't have felt more relieved or prouder.

The marathon had taken about 30 minutes longer than I'd anticipated and I was a little upset that I'd slowed down so much in the last 7 or so kilometers. However, I was also grateful that I was able to finish and knew I needed to focus on that. Besides, all things considered, it was still a respectable time.

I realized that sometimes a race isn't about time; it's about crossing both the starting line and the finish line, and that I certainly did!

17

We walked through the finish line gauntlet of volunteers, collecting our medals and heat sheets. Then we headed towards the checked gear pick-up points. Clinton's gear was waiting a few hundred meters farther up the line than mine, so we made a plan to get our gear, change and then meet back up and then head back to our hotel.

He wasn't out of sight for more than a minute when my emotions got the better of me. I fought back the tears until I saw a couple of other men doubled over and full-on crying. I wasn't alone in my feelings of accomplishment and I wasn't the only one who had just fought a battle. We all had on some level or another.

I sat down hard on the pavement and let the tears flow. Not since my childhood and my experience hobbling around the school track on crutches for the fundraiser had I felt so proud. I'd repeatedly been told that this was something I could never do. However, it clearly was; I just had to believe in myself.

I fumbled my phone out of my bag and called my estranged wife. My health and running had improved on the lead up to the New York City Marathon, but our relationship had not. However, she knew the blood, sweat and tears that I'd put into getting myself to this place and I needed to hear her voice. I secretly hoped that she, too, was proud of me.

I'd barely said hello before she told me what I needed to hear.

Clinton and I at the finish line of the New York City Marathon.

PART III

Making Lemonade

PUNE, INDIA 2018

It's 3:29AM and I'm staring at my phone, waiting for the alarm to go off in the next minute. I'm not a fan of waking up at this time of day unless it's just to roll over and fall back asleep. However, today is very different and I'm eager to get up.

I'm in Pune, India and in a few hours I'll be giving a speech to about 1,500 runners, then joining them for the LSOM – the Last Sunday of the Month race. I'm so excited to be running a local race that I somehow managed to forget about my speech.

Running in a foreign city or country is what I live for. The more exotic or further from the usual, the better. On this day, my girlfriend Jazmin and I will be the only two non-locals in the entire group but that's where our differences will end. Running is amazing like that as it doesn't matter where you're from, what language you speak, or what your social status or ability is. Runners share a common bond. Whatever race you run around this beautiful blue marble of ours, you'll always feel in the company of friends and family. Today would be no exception.

2

We're standing outside our rented apartment, watching the humongous bats circling overhead and waiting for our ride. The air feels surprisingly cold on my skin so I check the temperature and am shocked that it's already 24 degrees Celsius. I look at the forecast which said it would be a hot, sticky 40 degrees Celsius and I'm a little more grateful that it's an early morning race. By around the time the sun rises, we should already be finished and heading back.

We speed off to the event in a three-wheeled rickshaw. However, as we burn around corners and blow through red lights and stop signs, it feels like we're using only two of those wheels.

The streets are surprisingly busy at this early hour and not just with vehicles. Cows, pigs, camels and wild dogs are everywhere. However, after just a few days here we're already accustomed to seeing them in the streets. It's part of the appeal of this beautiful country.

3

As we near the venue a parking attendant greets us. A broad smile spreads across his face as if he recognizes me. He says that he'll call someone to properly receive us. At first, I assume this is typical protocol, but when we're 'properly received' a minute or so later, I'm almost positive the person called me by name. I'm about to ask Jazmin if I'm hearing things when someone else comes up, definitely calls me by name, and asks if they can take a photo with me.

I oblige, smiling for the photo with a confused look on my face. Not a moment later, another person asks for another photo. Soon I realize that everyone seems to know me. Later, I'd learn that my photo and bio had been sent out to the entire group of runners.

I'm introduced to running officials, the race organizers, the chief of police, the master of ceremonies and many others. I try to keep their names straight in my head. Meanwhile, even more people come up, greet me by name and introduce themselves. More of them ask to take pictures with me while others just snap a photo from a few feet away. It's overwhelming and exciting at the same time.

4

The night before I might have slept two hours but most likely less. I should be dead tired, but I've never felt more awake or pumped up. My head has been spinning the last few days as I try to wrap my head around why I'm really in India. I've received the opportunity to be the one and only authorized tour partner for all of India for perhaps the biggest marathon on the planet.

That's just me and my small company taking on a population closing in on 1.5 billion people. Within a few short weeks, I'm already neck-deep in meetings, contracts and new opportunities like the one presented to me this morning.

However, this morning my job is to give an inspiring speech, share my past struggles with my leg and foot and discuss why I started running. It has nothing to do with my new contract or with selling. Honestly, I'm both delighted to leave that behind and honored that they feel my story is inspiring. Of course, selling is important, and that time will come, but today is all about the sport that got me where I am today.

5

It's still full dark but the flood lamps in the distance illuminate the people as they arrive. A small crowd has formed close to the stage but still nowhere near the expected 1500. It's a bit of a relief and disappointment at the same time.

People are trying to pull me in a few different directions when the race organizers get my attention, then pull me to a quiet spot to explain what's required of me, what they now want from my speech. And now, they tell me that they want me to officially start the race.

With all the attention I'd completely forgotten about my speech again. My plan had been to think about what I wanted to say just before going on stage, but with all that was going on, it slipped my mind.

I've given many speeches over the years and to groups of different sizes but never to 1500 people, assuming they will all show up. I feel like I have to get away, even for just a minute, to clear my head and think about the words I want to share. It's important to me to give them some inspirational words before they head off on their race. I certainly don't want to disappoint them.

I look around for a place to rehearse but there's no time as more people want to meet me and I don't want to turn anyone away.

6

Just a few moments before I'm called onto the stage, I catch a much-needed 30 seconds to prepare. I look around at all the faces and realize that this group of people look the same as all the other groups of people I've spoken to in Canada. They're all here for the same reasons. We all have our personal demons, challenges and "why's" that brought us here. It doesn't matter whether we come from the same place or background, participate in the same running group or have the same lifestyle. We are all runners and share that communality and love of the sport, whether it's our first race or our hundredth. I know they will understand me even if my challenges are different from theirs because on some level, they will be able to relate.

I realize that I don't have to worry about the speech anymore; I simply need to speak from the heart.

I take another look around and realize just how fortunate I am to be here, to have the opportunity to speak to this group of people. I feel gooseflesh crawling up my arms and neck and I can't help but smile.

As I'm beaming with gratitude, I hear my name called. All eyes are on me as I make my way to the front of the crowd and onto the stage.

7

The emcee is doing a wonderful job, speaking in both English and Hindi. I'm certain the English is for my benefit only and I'm grateful once more. She finishes introducing me and hands me the microphone.

I walk to the front of the stage and look out at the sea of faces, all looking back at me. There's little doubt now that all 1,500 expected runners have shown up but somehow, I feel very relaxed and calm.

I remember back to when I first started instructing running programs for The Running Room in Edmonton, Alberta, almost 22 years ago. Truth be told, I agreed to teach those running classes not because of my love of running, but because of my fear of public speaking. I figured the best way to beat the fear was to face it head on. And, just like 22 years ago when I first stepped in front of a group of waiting faces, I realized that if one spoke about something which they are passionate about, there's nothing to fear.

8

I give my speech and it feels very natural despite not having engaged in public speaking for quite a while, and never for such a large group. While I address the group, I see knowing eyes looking back at me when I speak of overcoming challenges and life's obstacles. I'm touching a nerve because everyone there is dealing with something, large or small.

I feel a little overwhelmed and again, very grateful to have received the honor of speaking to this large group of runners. I incorporate the Martin Luther King Jr. quote which had gotten me running in the first place. This wins a large round of applause. Then I conclude my speech and thank them for giving me the honor and opportunity, as that's exactly how I feel.

I leave the stage and am greeted by someone I met just the day before. Pravin Zele is holding the 60-minute pacer sign for the 10K race – a slow and easy pace for him despite the fact that he runs barefoot. Pravin will be inducted into *The Guinness Book of World Records* for running 121 half marathons in 121 consecutive days, barefoot. He had started running barefoot simply because he refused to let the fact that he couldn't afford running shoes stop him from doing what he loved. Now he's being offered huge endorsements by a major shoe company to wear their product – which, naturally, he turned down. He won't ever run in shoes again and why would he? He runs for love of the sport, not the money he's accustomed to living without. People like Pravin inspire me and fire me up to run. I wonder why he wasn't on the stage instead of me.

Standing in his presence gives me such a boost and now I'm the one who wants a photo. As I turn to ask him for a picture, I'm pulled in another direction, shaking more hands and wondering again why anyone would be interested in my story when people like Pravin are here.

Pravin Zele and I the day before the LSOM run

9

It's still dark when I blow the whistle announcing the start of the race. I watch the faces of the runners as they surge forward together, all seeming to smile. Some high-five me as they run past while others call out my name. I take a few minutes to enjoy the moment, then pass off the whistle and join the back of the pack.

Jazmin and I start off, running alongside the fast-moving traffic with scooters and motorbikes weaving in between the runners, then turn off into a quiet suburb where instead of motorbikes, cows are weaving amongst the runners.

I'm impressed by the fantastic race crew who are offering all the staples of a major race. Clearly, they've been doing this for years.

I assume my 15 minutes of fame are up but runners continue calling out to me as we run, filling me with more energy. I feel incredible despite the fact that I barely slept the night before.

10

I turn to Jazmin to see if she's enjoying herself; it's obvious that she is. She's beaming just like I am. I note our quick pace despite the heat and the fact that we're running up a steep hill that seems endless. However, that doesn't seem to matter to her and it definitely doesn't matter to me. I feel like I'm floating!

We make quick eye contact and I ask her if she's ready. She nods and throws me a crazy runner's grin that says it all. We find a new gear and fly up the hill.

Pune Speech

Running in New Delhi

Chapter 9 – Mad for the Marathon

I remember swearing up and down during that long, hard stretch of road between 32 and 40 kilometers during the New York City Marathon that I would never, ever run another marathon. And I meant it. Running a marathon was ridiculous, hard on the body, and torture to my foot and leg. Why would I ever want to subject myself to that again? It made no sense.

Yet, somewhere along those last two kilometers of the course, amongst the throngs of screaming spectators and high-fiving children, something shifted in me. Yes, the race was brutal on my body and yes, it hurt like hell and yes, I swore that I would never, ever do that again. But...

But that feeling of crossing the finish line after all the preparation and dedication to the training, the pain I had to go through and the weight loss was beyond incredible! I felt an overwhelming sense of accomplishment and self-satisfaction that's incredibly difficult to explain or understand unless you experience it firsthand. It's also the realization that we are capable of far more than we'll ever understand.

It was partly this deep realization that rocked me hard and brought me to tears post-marathon.

Before this marathon I had never tested myself so much. Rather, I had hidden in the shadows of my fears and doubts. However, just a taste of what I was capable of doing was enough to make me want to test myself more.

I realized that I was much more than the sum of my past experiences. I was capable of more than I gave myself credit for and my only real limits were those I imposed upon myself … and I didn't need to impose any. I also realized that I dictated my own reality and that my reality was nothing more than the projections of my mindset. If I thought I wasn't capable of doing another marathon, I wasn't. However, if I thought that I was capable, I definitely was.

So yes, I had sworn that I would never run another marathon, but that was only the pain and self-doubt talking. That wasn't me.

2

I don't think Clinton and I had managed to get halfway back to our hotel after the marathon before we started talking about which marathon would be next. It started off as a joke, like, "Geez, let's do that again someday," before the laughter slowly turned to a nervous, knowing chuckle. This then turned into Clinton asking if I had been to Iceland. I hadn't, I said, but had always wanted to go. I asked if Iceland had a marathon. Clinton winked, assuring me it did.

3

I had assumed that the pain I'd felt while running would end once I crossed the finish line. Of course, that's not how it works. It doesn't work like that for anyone, especially those of us who are dealing with additional grievances or disabilities.

However, all the pain that followed the marathon was nothing more to me than a constant reminder of my accomplishment. Every wince, painful set of stairs or attempt to sit on the toilet was followed by a smile.

During the marathon my ankle and foot had swollen significantly. However, the inflammation was lessening every day. Two weeks after the marathon, I was finally walking as normal as normal gets for me.

4

Waiting two full weeks to run again while my body worked its way back to its version of normal was difficult. I'd wanted to get back out there as soon as possible but I also wanted to give my body the chance to properly recover.

Once the two weeks were up, I returned to my regular routine of running the five-kilometer loop around my neighborhood and pushing the limits on my Sunday long runs. I continued losing weight and improving my run times. I also continued to note that my ankle and foot were strengthening. At some point I had learned to run with my foot angled outwards which aligned my leg a little better, thus taking the pressure off it and my hip.

A month later and about five months before leaving for Iceland, I returned to the Running Room once more and enrolled in another marathon program. Once again, I was surprised at how much more I learned about a sport that seemed so simple but was far from it.

Marathon training went even better the second time and my leg, ankle and foot seemed better than it had during the first training program. They still hurt, they were still constantly swollen, but either they were getting stronger, or I was simply getting accustomed to the pain. Either way, I was pleased with the training and how I was handling it.

Then, before I knew it, I was once again traveling for a race: my second marathon and fourth race.

5

Running the Reykjavik Marathon was a very different experience than running the New York

City Marathon. In Iceland we were able to start at the very front of the pack, only an arm's length from the world's fastest runners. On the other hand, in New York, it had taken us about 10 minutes to cross the starting line once the race officially started. And rather than three million spectators lining the course, Reykjavik had perhaps 300. The two races couldn't have been more different.

As in the New York City Marathon, my right foot and ankle gave me substantial grief. Despite strengthening over the course of training for both marathons, the inability to fully recover after each long run eventually took its toll and I was definitely feeling it on the marathon.

Like that first marathon, however, I also came prepared with my pain killers. To avoid consuming double-digit pills like I did in New York, I brought only six pills to Iceland as I was determined to wean myself off them. It just didn't seem like the way to get through a marathon.

6

If you've ever met me on a racecourse or spent some time knocking off the miles with me, odds are you've heard one of the many stories that motivate me to keep going. These stories are about various personal heroes of mine who have overcome amazing obstacles to beat unbelievable odds. They inspire me a lot and I love sharing them with others in the hopes that doing so will not only inspire both of us while running, but also take my mind off both the race and the pain.

I was fortunate that during the Reykjavik Marathon I met a couple of women who were running the same pace I was and who were also part of the charity group for which I was running. After some small chit chat I asked them if it would be OK to share one of these stories. They agreed and I proceeded to drag out a five-minute story over the course of around 10 kilometers. I'm not sure if they enjoyed hearing it as much as I enjoyed sharing it, but it definitely made the marathon go by a lot quicker. Well, for me, anyways.

At the end of this story and before I finally left them in peace, one of the women asked me what I did for pain. By that point in the marathon, roughly around the 25-kilometer mark, I had consumed four of my six painkillers and was ready to take the last two. However, I was concerned about the later kilometers when I would really need them.

Without thinking, I offered her my last two pills, wished them luck and ran ahead before I could change my mind and beg for one or both of them back. Once that initial feeling of 'what did I just do' passed, I made myself a promise that I would never take anything again for pain management. Instead, I would accept the pain and use it as a tool to understand that my body was simply telling me something. Instead of muting it, I would listen and try to fix the problem. No more Band-Aid solutions.

7

Although I experienced a substantial amount of pain while finishing that marathon, I realized it was still tolerable and that I didn't need the pills. It turned out that I had made the right decision, and this further solidified my decision to never take them again. And I never have.

8

Unlike the New York City Marathon, Clinton and I only started together in Iceland. He had amped up his training in a way I could only dream of. He had also lost a lot of weight and was focused on speed whereas I was happy to simply finish the marathon, although I did try to cut at least a little time off. And as it would turn out, I did and considerably.

Despite the lack of crowd support and painkillers, I used my previous technique of choosing an object in the distance and running towards it with the promise that I would walk a little once I got to it. However, once I got there,

I instantly chose another object and ran towards that with another promise to allow myself a short break if required. By constantly allowing myself the chance to rest if required, I nickel and dimed myself all the way to the finish line without walking.

I ran through the finish line and the small but enthusiastic crowd of supporters, beating my New York time by about 30 minutes. I couldn't have been happier. Number two was now in the books.

We flew home, medals proudly hanging from our necks, and once again we started thinking about the next marathon.

9

By this point, my family started realizing that this wasn't some sort of fad and that I was truly hooked on running. They were interested in supporting me at a race, but I didn't think they were so interested that they would travel overseas with me or into the US. Wanting to taste the idea of having my own personal cheer squad, I decided to run my third marathon in Edmonton, Alberta.

Once again, I joined a training program at the Running Room and once again I learned much more about this sport that was becoming a serious part of me.

10

The Race the Twilight Marathon in Edmonton started at 5PM which was a real change from the typical early-morning start that most marathons use. I preferred it and it also worked well for my family who all turned up to support me.

Once again, I bested my previous marathon but this time, I did so painkiller-free. It wasn't easy and many times throughout the course I regretted not having pills, but afterwards I was very grateful for my decision as it proved that the painkillers weren't necessary, only desired.

It made for my third marathon when I crossed the finish line that day, and all three were completed in just under 10 months.

Chapter 10 – The Birth of Dream Travel Canada

During those ten months and three marathons I made a monumental number of positive changes in my life. I had quit my six-figure career, separated from my wife, lost 75 pounds and sold my house and absolutely all my possessions with the exceptions of my clothes (those that still fit), my computer and my desk. Essentially, I left with the same things with which I had entered my relationship eight years earlier.

Despite flipping my life upside down, I felt much happier and a lot lighter and not just physically. With no work or anything else to worry about, I took off to Europe to both find myself and figure out what I wanted to do next.

Perhaps I should have been stressed or at least concerned about making money or where I was going to live when I returned from my trip, but honestly, I'd never felt better.

I knew that everything would work out as it always seemed to do. Besides, I had some cash and a ridiculous amount of credit. I was marketable and I certainly wasn't afraid of hard work. That said, I also knew that I had to find something that made me happy as I didn't want to go through another life reset another 10 years down the road. Instead, I vowed to find something that brought meaning to my life, that made me want to get out of bed each morning and that made me truly happy.

It would be my dream job, but I had no idea what that looked like. However, rather than worrying about it, I enjoyed my travels while focusing on the two things I enjoyed most: traveling and running.

2

For years I had been running in Edmonton which boasts the highest number of kilometers of running trails within the city limits of any city in North America. That makes for some fantastic running. However, when you're running between 100 and 150 kilometers a week, you quickly burn through all the trails the city has to offer. As much as I love running in the River Valley there, it's amazing to discover a new city by simply dropping your gear at a hotel, slapping on the running shoes and heading out. That said, by that point in my life my traveling was usually limited to where my job took me, which was mostly around Northern Alberta but that was about to change in a big way.

I had turned my two-month European trip into two years of almost back-to-back trips, going on three- and four-week vacations at a time. However, I felt that it wasn't quite enough. I wanted to lose the restrictions and simply travel but my money was running out and I knew that I had to find work.

I had picked up the odd job when I wasn't traveling but the jobs always quickly escalated into a possible career path. It turned out that being young with many years of upper retail management experience goes a long way. However, I got bored quickly and constantly turned down promotions even though they meant very good money. I turned them down because somehow, I knew they simply weren't the right path for me. I didn't want to fall back into another 10-year position with a company that didn't value me or maintain the same values I did.

3

I had just quit another job that offered me a promotion and a starting salary of $80,000, with a corner office and the works because they wouldn't give me two weeks off to go to Mexico on a pre-arranged trip with a friend. That sounds crazy to most, I'm sure, but what good is that sort of money and position if you're working for a company that felt it acceptable to dangle a promotion while canceling your holidays? It was the exact same type of power move that I'd dealt with during my 10-year, retail management position. Honestly, it simply made my decision easy and I ended up having a great time in Mexico.

Shortly after coming back, I came across a Help Wanted sign for a part-time job at my local Running Room. I went inside, met the store manager and worked hard to convince her that I really did want to work part-time despite my previous work experience.

I loved the simplicity of the position and the fact that I could help people run. Perhaps I wouldn't make what I was previously making but I would be absolutely stress-free, make enough to support my lifestyle and be constantly surrounded by people who inspired me.

4

I got the job and before long I was instructing running programs while also working the sales floor. I was in absolute heaven and never once looked back at where I'd come from or how much I'd previously made. In fact, I was one of three part-time workers at that location who had been making six figures before working for the Running Room part-time. Clearly, we all felt the same way about the importance of quality of life. I didn't need the extra validation, but it didn't hurt to see that I wasn't absolutely crazy – or, at least, the only crazy one.

I was proud of my new home and family at the Running Room and I couldn't have been happier. Although I didn't know it at the time, my taking a step down in pay and following my heart had caused the wheels of destiny to quickly turn in my favor and my dream job started to materialize.

5

Having a steady stream of income and a stress-free life freed me up to consider my next steps. I knew that traveling and running were two keys to my happiness, but by working at the Running Room I found that helping others was also very important to me.

It was then that I realized that my dream job was as simple as marrying those three things.

It seemed like such a simple concept and yet it was very powerful to me. It just made sense. I immediately went to work sorting out the details.

As my running class and I met three times a week for group runs, I decided to ask them what they thought about the idea of training together for a race, then traveling there as a group and running it together. The response was overwhelming, and the idea of Dream Travel Canada was born.

6

Putting together running groups made perfect sense. I had the business background to create the company, but I had no idea about booking travel, nor did I want to rely on another company. I had already run two foreign marathons by going through local companies and had been thoroughly disappointed. If I was going to start my own company, I felt it had to be done properly. Therefore, I enrolled in a travel program and went back to school at the age of 29.

Many people in my life hadn't understood why I would leave a 10-year, six-figure income at the age of 26 with plenty of room for advancement. However, after they saw how happy I was afterwards they no longer questioned my decision. So, when they heard I was going back to school and starting my own business, they didn't question it either. They supported me and my dream.

7

Within a few short months of graduating from the travel program I had officially started my business and had scheduled my first marathon group to go to Africa. We were heading to

Tanzania to run a marathon, hike Kilimanjaro and finish with a safari on the Serengeti.

It ended up being an epic trip and one that I still offer today and go on myself occasionally.

My second trip, already in the works when I was escorting the group to Tanzania, was to the New York City Marathon. Though it was two years after I'd initially suggested it to my running group, most of them still made the trip and ran their first marathon with me.

Dream Travel Canada had just barely started and already it was a success.

8

I quickly graduated from working under the banner of another agency while finishing up the travel program to starting my own office and hiring my own staff. I had to let my sales position with the Running Room go, however, I was able to continue as a running instructor, which I still do today, only now for their online programs.

Within a year or so, Dream Travel Canada was offering running vacations to the Great Wall of China, Machu Picchu, Mt. Kilimanjaro, New York City, Disneyland and Disney World, and a host of other places. Clearly, the idea of traveling the world and running races was something that resonated with others.

In an effort to create a better quality of life by breaking free of the rat race and giving up on everything towards which I'd previously worked, I found my calling and my dream job. When it came time to think of a business name, it wasn't hard at all. I chose the first name that came to me as it really meant something important. Eighteen years later, Dream Travel Canada is still my dream job, and I couldn't be happier.

Dream Travel's first expo booth

New look, new logo, still bald

Chapter 11 – Tackling the Gobi March

I've never fancied myself to be a great runner nor even a mediocre runner. I run because I love the sport. I definitely appreciate the challenge of it as well as the constant reminder that I'm very fortunate to even be able to do it.

However, that feeling of being challenged tends to slip a little, especially after running 10 or so marathons, which by then I'd done. Of course, I could have challenged myself to run a marathon faster but that was never my game as I preferred distance over velocity. Besides, I wasn't exactly born for speed. Some days I wonder if that has more to do with my love of food than it does with my foot and leg issues.

Because distance was my thing, an ultra would have made perfect sense but I honestly wasn't exposed to any. Between being relatively new to the sport, busy building and growing my business and instructing running programs, I hadn't had a real opportunity.

Then, during a lull at work one day in 2007 while leafing through a running magazine I'd picked up on a whim, an opportunity finally presented itself.

2

For the first time since I'd started my business, I had a business partner which meant I was free to leave the office, go offline and start taking advantage of being a business owner. It was exciting and I was looking forward to finding a race off the beaten path, something that would challenge me. However, of all the articles in the magazine, the one that caught my attention seemed to be a joke at first glance – some sort of 'could you imagine if...' race. However, it wasn't a joke and I read on with both amazement and fear. I realized that my heart was speeding up, then it proceeded to jackhammer in my chest. I was looking for a new adventure, but I was thinking of something like a race in a place like Namibia, not something that could possibly kill me. Yet as I read on, I knew I had to do it. I had to do it because it scared me half to death.

Ever since I was a child, I'd had a funny thing with fear. Fear of the dark? OK, so let's go downstairs into the basement, which was a mouse- and bat-infested, wall-less dirt hole in the ground beneath our house, turn off the lights and see why I was so scared. Afraid of what was lurking under my bed? Guess I'll be sleeping there tonight to ensure it's only my imagination. Run a six-day, 250+ kilometer race through the "world's least hospitable landscape" with 35 pounds on my back, extreme heat and rationed water? Guess I'll be heading to China to run the Gobi March.

It seemed so ridiculous and unbelievable that it scared me beyond comprehension. I simply had to run it.

Perhaps more than anything, it was the idea of running back-to-back-to-back marathons when I had repeatedly read that one should run only four marathons a year, at most, to prevent injury and allow the body to fully recover between races. I just couldn't conceive of the idea of having to run the equivalent of six marathons in six days and under the harshest of conditions. It seemed crazy.

Yet, that's how the Gobi March is set up. The course is "roughly" a marathon a day for four days straight, the fifth day a mere "80-100" kilometers, depending, and then the sixth day a nice little 10-kilometer leg-stretcher. Distances were rough because the race staff literally mapped the course the day before.

To make the race even more difficult, runners had to carry their own food, cooking utensils, medical supplies, clothes, toilet paper, books and whatever else they wanted or needed for the entire six days, while running. Runners would receive enough water to get through the first leg of Day One. Then they would receive additional water at every checkpoint, which could be a good number of kilometers away, depending on the terrain. That rationed water would be used to not only drink but cook dehydrated food over an open fire, bathe and potentially wash clothes.

Basically, this event went against everything I had ever learned about running, yet all this ridiculousness intrigued me. The race started way off the grid in an extremely remote part of Western China, somewhere I had never been – somewhere that most people had never been – and ran into seemingly uncharted parts of the country. As a bonus, the race was also just 13 days after the Great Wall of China Marathon, which I had also always wanted to run, meaning I could potentially get in both races during one trip.

I was already thinking ahead. Too far ahead, maybe. I was picturing myself there, running it alongside some of the world's greatest runners, through that incredibly picturesque countryside, so far from civilization. I had done this type of visualization before and knew that when I started engaging in it, running the race was a foregone conclusion.

3
I read on, already knowing that I was going to run this race yet realizing that so much was unknown about it including things I considered relatively important like the actual distance and location of the race. The article spoke of rough locations but nothing specific and indicated that everything depended on several factors that would change yearly.

The exact race distance was unknown as the race officials – two incredibly courageous ultra-runners – headed out and marked each day's route about 24 hours before the participants ran it. They had an idea where the course would start and end and that it would be roughly 250 kilometers, but whatever happened between those two points was determined by what those two ultra-runners decided at the time.

It all seemed awesomely cruel. I felt goose flesh crawling up my arms and neck as I read on.

4
My mind was reeling with thoughts, both positive and negative, about such an event.

Things like the risk factors, logistics and cost. I had started reading the article mostly to kill a slow afternoon in the office but something in the back of my mind realized that something much bigger was going on. It was one of those great opportunities in life that present themselves. I was caught somewhere between the discovery and acceptance of that opportunity.

I went to the organizer's website to 'take a peek' and somehow accidentally filled in my information, clicked on *Register* and placed a hefty, non-refundable deposit. I did it all on autopilot and I'm pretty sure I didn't breathe during the entire registration process. Had I taken a moment to breathe, I would have had a moment to think. Had that been the case, reasoning would have taken over and I would have thrown my computer out the window and run the other way.

5

Once the hard part was done and I was officially registered for a race well beyond my ability, I allowed reasoning to set in. I was clearly in over my head, but I also trusted that everything would work out exactly as it had to; it always did.

Since I figured everything would work out and since I was already abusing my credit card, I decided that I'd better register for the Great Wall of China Marathon as well. As hard as that race was going to be, it would serve as my final taper run before the Gobi March which I would run less than two weeks later.

6

Owning a travel agency dedicated to taking runners and walkers to different races around the world seemed like the perfect reason to build a tour around the Great Wall Marathon and offer it to my clients. So, that's exactly what I did.

At some point I thought about looking into the possibility of selling clients into the Gobi March as well but I really wanted to keep it just for myself. Besides, I didn't think it smart to run a six-day, 250+ kilometer race in the desert, without the ability to shower for a week while worrying about my clients' health and well-being at the same time. It wouldn't be fair to them or me.

I decided to keep the Gobi March for myself and got busy building packages to the Great Wall of China Marathon, hoping it would be a success like my other events.

7

Signing up for a race like the Gobi March meant

finding a specialized training program. At the time there was no shortage of training programs for the typical, one day ultras, but finding something that would work for the Gobi didn't seem to exist.

In the end, I decided to use the same principles from the Running Room marathon schedule but beefed up, and of course, with a weighted backpack. I determined what my peak week of running should look like and then built my schedule backwards.

8

Running with a backpack is extremely awkward but will do wonders for anyone's race times eventually.

I had first started using it only to hold a change of clothes. Even then, I was certain I'd never get up to the 30 pounds for which I'd aimed while training. Even with such minimal weight the backpack constantly flopped around or pulled on my shoulders making it very uncomfortable to run. It was so uncomfortable and foreign that I decided that I would have to alter my training plan, at least when it came to my backpack, as there was just no way that 30lbs was going to work.

Instead of planning to build up to 30lbs in my backpack, a pack that I would use on every single training run throughout my entire training program, I decided that I needed to get up to 40lbs. I determined that the more I suffered during training the less I would in China. Besides, it hadn't been that long before that I was carrying an extra 75lbs. The only difference was where it was located, and I was grateful that I could at least take the bag off at the end of each run.

Little by little I started adding more weight. At first it was a change of clothes and a second pair of running shoes. Then it was the same but with a 5lb weight wrapped up in a towel to prevent it from banging into my back. Then it was a 10lb weight, then it was multiple weights.

I was pleasantly surprised at how quickly I adapted and the feeling of having something so heavy and uncomfortable strapped to my back slowly dissipated.

Everywhere I ran, I did so with that bag. It didn't matter if I was on a training run, running to my sister's house for dinner or running other races during my training, I still ran with my weighted bag. Just a few months into training I ran a marathon in Mississippi with around 25lbs in my backpack and to the surprise of both myself and other runners. More than a few came up to me on the course and asked what I was up to. I tried explaining to the first few people that just two weeks earlier I'd run another marathon but hadn't been allowed to run with a backpack so I wanted to find a marathon that I could run with it. That didn't seem to make much sense to them, and I can't say I blamed them. None of what I was doing really made sense to me, either.

There were just a couple of times that I took off the bag for a five-kilometer race and both times I was both impressed and surprised at how quickly I ran without it. Both races ended up being a new personal best. In fact, I started to realize that I could start placing at some local events, assuming none of the real speed demons showed up, if I continued to focus on 5K races and without my bag.

To me that was pretty incredible. Here I was, still new to running having made it through a few marathons and still struggling with some pain and discomfort, and now I could win some local 5K races.

Running 5K's, however, was not what I was interested in, nor was winning races. Don't get me wrong, winning a race would have been fantastic, but I knew that I needed to focus on distance. Besides, winning a race would have meant that someone didn't show up that day. There's always someone faster and trying to focus on padding my ego wouldn't serve me for long. Instead, I remained focused on my ultra.

During my training I became obsessed about running everywhere with my bag. It was my friend and we were inseparable. Even when I was invited to a friend's place, I would first ask them if I could shower upon arrival as I would be running to and from their place and not driving. It was a strange and difficult request at first but eventually it became a habit and everyone always supported me.

When I wasn't running I was in the gym, lifting weights, running stairs with a large weighted bag across my shoulders, swimming and taking spin classes. I ate, slept, breathed and lived training for almost an entire year. I had never been in such great shape and I was very proud of my strength and the fact that I had finally started taking my nutrition seriously by cutting back considerably on all the previous garbage I was eating. Even my leg and foot seemed to be keeping up with me for the most part.

However, I still looked overweight due to inflammation from Crohn's Disease. More importantly, however, I stayed very healthy and injury-free which allowed me to push myself to new limits.

9
Despite staying healthy and not having any major Crohn's attacks, the inflammation really

bothered me. I weighed in the neighborhood of 180 pounds yet looked like I weighed around 220. It seemed that no matter how well I ate, I constantly battled extreme inflammation. To be honest, it was embarrassing and annoying.

When I sidelined my ego and focused on what I had done, I felt that I was making great improvements. Eventually, my confidence grew with it. I had been embarking on an adventure of which I was actually worthy. I no longer thought of myself as a fake who had somehow snuck into an event meant for the super elite as I had when I first registered.

My body was holding up and so were my right leg and foot. I was shocked at my ability to put on such incredible mileage that previously would have scared me almost as much as the race had when I first read about it. Even during my final week of heavy running, when I hit 190 kilometers in one week, my foot and leg only bothered me as much as they had during the training for my previous marathon.

10

Although I had registered for the ultra-marathon and the Great Wall of China Marathon a good year in advance, the time passed extremely quickly. Before I knew it I was flying to China with my clients for our two-week tour of China prior to running on the Great Wall.

I'm grateful that the ultra hadn't overshadowed my trip with my clients or the Great Wall Marathon as it was something I'd always dreamed of doing. I ended up running the marathon with my friend, the backpack, with around 30 pounds, and turned in one of my slowest-ever marathon times. In the process I lost my remaining five toenails, for which I was grateful, as it would make the ultra that much easier.

11

After my group tour of China, I said my goodbyes to my clients in Hong Kong, then headed 4,000 kilometers west to the city of Kashgar on the far Western side of China.

Kashgar is a remarkable city if you like off-the-beaten-path, historical types of places that see very few tourists. A rustic beauty, bordered by mountains and desert, it was as far from home as I could have imagined.

I checked into my hotel which seemed oddly deserted considering it was the host hotel for the event. After dropping my gear in my room, I headed out to explore.

Upon my return a few hours later, I found the previously quiet hotel overflowing with runners, gear, volunteers and staff members running around and organizing the international group of overly excited runners. It was like I'd stepped into another dimension, one that allowed the ramifications of my actions to quickly catch up to me.

Until that morning I'd been mostly relaxed and not really concerned about the race. However, that quickly changed once I saw the hotel full of runners. Those months of training, thousands of kilometers and killing off more pairs of running shoes than I can remember, it hit me hard. The early bedtimes, the extreme dietary changes, the sacrifices, the time and money I'd invested in getting there all hit me. There I was, in the middle of nowhere, on the far side of the planet, surrounded by other equally crazy people who had also sacrificed so much to make this a reality.

I looked around, completely bewildered. There wasn't a place to sit in the entire lobby, as enormous as it was. A pile of luggage that started in a far corner had spilled outwards, eating up a quarter of the lobby. People were scattered about, sitting wherever they could find space, whether it was on a chair, the floor or their luggage.

I heard Spanish, German, French, Italian and a host of other languages I couldn't place. Ages ranged from surprisingly young to surprisingly old. There was such a mix of people, but everyone seemed to have the same dumbfounded smile dominating their faces. It was impossible to not smile, even with all the fear behind it. We had worked our tails off to be there and spent a small fortune each. We'd made our way to the other side of the world to a place that few tourists would ever reach. We were an eclectic group of runners about to participate in one of the planet's most difficult running events.

I took a deep breath and a long look around the lobby. Through the organized chaos I realized that I was standing in the middle of some of the greatest distance runners known today.

12

The next 18 hours were a blur as we dealt with check-in procedures, heard the rules of the race, reviewed safety considerations, signed waivers and proved that we had each brought a sufficient number of calories for the entire six-day race. Although everything was important, the race organizers really made a point of ensuring that we brought enough calories. It didn't matter how you got the calories in as long as they added up to at least the minimum required amount.

I had been impressed with my choices for lightweight, calorie-dense food until I saw a group of Italians who showed up with almost nothing more than bottles of olive oil. It blew my mind but at the same time made a ton of sense. Their bottles of oil, weighing maybe four pounds per person, gave them basically the same number of calories that were in my 20 pounds of food. It was genius, but only if you could stomach consuming virtually nothing but oil for six days.

I decided that, heavy or not, I was fine with my choice of dehydrated, space station-inspired powdered foods.

When everything was said and done, and after we'd signed our waivers and the organizers had weighed everyone's backpacks to see who had the lightest and who was the sucker with the heaviest, we were left to explore the city or get some rest in the hotel before our early departure the following morning.

I chose to head up to my room and see what I could eliminate from my gear since I was that sucker with the heaviest backpack.

13
Early the following morning we were divided into small groups and driven out of town in 4x4s

to an autonomous zone roughly four hours north of Kashgar. It was a beautiful, awe-inspiring, bumpy trip from the edge of nowhere to parts completely unknown.

As our vehicles approached our destination, locals lined the dusty road and cheered our arrival. They danced for us, sang and lined up to be in our photos. They shook our hands, patted us on the backs and made us feel like we had already completed the race.

This was where we would spend our first night in the desert and which also would act as our first staging area. In the distance the starting area was already set up, beckoning and teasing us. However, first there was a welcoming party to attend.

We were the guests of honor in a place that, we were told, had never previously received foreigners. It was an honor and privilege to share the last few hours with them before heading off into insanity.

The sucker and his heavy backpack.

Photo with three women? Don't mind if I do!

14

We spent the balance of that day enjoying the
hospitality and then settling into the various
buildings that the locals had offered up that

night. The buildings consisted of a church, a makeshift school and the like, all of which had been around for easily a few hundred years. With stone walls and mosaic tile-laid floors, they constituted a desert oasis.

That first night I was bunked with famous long-distance runner Dean Karnazes. Being in such company was both an honor and terrifying. It was an honor as I had incredible respect for what he had accomplished in running and terrifying because it made me think again that perhaps I was in over my head.

We dined early on whatever dehydrated food we had each brought while the Italians cheered with glasses of olive oil. We had a chance to mingle a bit and I took advantage of the opportunity, meeting runners from all over the world including another famous long-distance runner from Brazil who had run 9,000 kilometers in 100 days while wearing Crocs. He was about to run the Gobi March in them as well. I met a reporter from CNN who was supposed to only cover the race but who, the day before it started, decided that the best way to cover such an event was to participate in it. I met many other equally amazing individuals.

15
Early the next morning we formed a large mob

at the starting line while the locals prepared to send us off with shouts, cheers and the banging of a gong. My heart raced while I took one last look around, trying to push away thoughts that I was just some wannabe runner mixed in with actual running celebrities.

I, too, deserve to be here, I thought. After double-digit marathons all over the world, I had put in almost a full year of specialized training for this event. I may not have been famous nor stood on any international podiums, but I certainly had the same will power and determination to tackle this race.

I started feeling a little more confident and tried to relax a little. Then, before I knew it, the banging of the gong became louder than the banging in my chest. Somewhere a gun went off and the crowd surged forward.

I took off way too quickly but felt as light as air despite most-likely still having the heaviest pack in the group. My smile broadened and I ran off into the desert with some of the world's greatest runners.

16

When I'd first read about the Gobi March a year earlier, while sitting in the safety and comfort of my office, I thought that perhaps the author had been exaggerating, embellishing the difficulty of the course, the heat or the obstacles runners encountered. On Day One I quickly came to realize that, if anything, the author had held back on some of the event's more torturous parts, perhaps to avoid scaring people off completely.

I don't think we were more than a kilometer or two into the race when we came across a river that had to be crossed, not once, not twice but more than 10 times. (I stopped counting after that.) The river had snaked wickedly in front of us and, rather than allowing us to run around it, the course ran purposely through each bend.

The first time we had to cross the river I stopped at the edge and started taking off my shoes while other runners ran past, splashing through, shoes and all. I quickly re-laced my shoes and did the same. The cold water on my hot skin felt fantastic.

The desert heat was so intense that by the time I reached the next river crossing less than a couple minutes later, my shoes and socks seemed mostly dry.

We ran on, crossing and recrossing that river. We ran up and over foothills, down through valleys, crossing more rivers or maybe the same one, all the while following little pink flags that the organizers had stuck in the ground every 100 meters or so.

We ran up and over more foothills, each noticeably larger than the last, then down their rocky slopes on the far sides, always with more desert ahead. We followed animal trails and motorbike tracks, but always with the little pink flags in sight. One wouldn't want to lose sight of them and get lost out there.

Six-and-a-half hours later, I crossed the finish line of Day One in the top 25 percent of runners. I felt great and my body didn't hurt at all. It seemed easier than any of my previous marathons despite the heavy backpack, heat and terrain.

Day One

17

Despite doing so well on Day One and being fine with the weight on my back, I decided it was time to dump out some more things as I knew that over six days I would experience a compounding effect.

Runners assumed that the race officials performed only the one bag and calorie check so many of us started throwing away non-essentials and extra food in an effort to lighten our loads. I threw away my spare pair of runners and all my powered sports drink. I squeezed out 90 percent of my toothpaste, ripped out half the empty pages in my journal and ditched the deodorant (it was obvious that it was useless...we all smelled after the first hour) and magazines I'd brought. I then donated all my clothes other than one pair of running shorts, one running shirt and one spare shirt in which to sleep. I even snapped off the handle on my toothbrush, like I saw others doing. I slashed and cut with reckless abandon but still ended up with roughly two-thirds of what I'd started with. My food simply weighed way too much.

That night we were given our official rooming list for the balance of the race. I was very fortunate to have been roomed with the Italians along with their constant optimism, smiles and laughter. We shared an eight-man tent and at the end of each day, none of us seemed to have any issues falling asleep on the hard ground. Despite Day One seeming relatively easy, we were all exhausted.

18

Day Two started with more freeze-dried food, our rationed water for drinking, cooking and a quick rinse and then the ceremonial banging of the gong to symbolize the start of the next 42 or so kilometers.

Starting out on the second day I felt confident even though just the day before I had run more than a full marathon and under hard conditions. My right leg and foot seemed to be holding up fine. They hurt, but that was the status quo. My only concern was that I hadn't urinated since the morning of Day One. Considering the heat, it was important to keep the body functioning correctly and a lack of urination was definitely a cause for concern. I made a mental note to drink more water.

I started Day Two with the CNN reporter and a military fellow, both of whom seemed tough as nails. The day was extremely hot and as we progressed the course became more difficult. There would be no rivers to cross on Day Two, but the course did take us up and over a series of eight large, daunting foothills that could have been mountains in disguise. Going up was fine but running along the rocky ridges and then coming down was quite treacherous. Many runners had fallen and cut open their palms and knees but continued on like the warriors they were. That said, it wasn't like they had an alternative; medical attention, except for in dire situations and only when the race officials somehow knew that someone required it, would be available only at the next checkpoint.

I was feeling good overall but after a few hours I still hadn't urinated. When I made it into the first checkpoint, as if reading my mind, one of the staff members asked me about the last time I'd gone. Apparently, what I was experiencing was common and the race organizers were on the lookout for it.

I assumed that telling the truth would slow me down. Therefore, I told them I'd gone just a few kilometers back. The truth was that it had been roughly 26 hours. Lying to the staff was a terrible mistake and one that I came to deeply regret.

After just a short break at the checkpoint tent, I ran off, assuming I could make the necessary adjustments to avoid bodily harm. I set my watch to beep every 10 minutes so that, thirsty or not, I'd take a sip of water. I hoped that would rectify the situation.

The three of us continued running together for a while, then eventually separated when I suggested they go on ahead. My body was starting to break down and I didn't want to hold them back.

When I was running on my own, I started to space out a bit and got mentally lost in the incredible scenery and my thoughts. I lost track of everything other than placing one foot in front of the other and following those little pink flags. The next time I heard my watch beep I was astonished to see that over seven hours had passed. I had been in a running trance, induced by following the pink flags in a sea of grey: grey sky, grey rocks and grey mountains.

I took some long, deep swigs from my warm bottles of water, but my body didn't seem to want it. It was already too late; I was dangerously dehydrated.

Despite being sick I pushed on, knowing I had to get to the next checkpoint while sipping as much water as I could. Sometime later, I I saw the CNN reporter who had finished the distance that day but had come back to find me. She figured that I needed help as I apparently looked pretty bad when she last saw me.

We shared a quick, tired hello before I asked her for some water. I had somehow managed to get two bottles of water into me but was now thirsty for more. Extremely thirsty.

It was against the rules to share food, supplies or water but I was beyond desperate.

She listened to me while I mumbled my words, barely coherent and while looking down at the two full bottles of water strapped into their holders at my waist. She asked me what was wrong with the water I had.

I must have looked like a fool because I couldn't see the water bottles she was referring to. I told her again that I was completely out when she pointed down to my water belt. I tried to follow her pointing hand, but it magically disappeared from my sight once it passed below my chest on my right side.

I had gone mostly blind in my right eye from severe dehydration. I should have been more concerned, but I was also heat and sun stroked so my head wasn't working all that well.

She realized I was in dire straits so grabbed my arm and ran back the remaining kilometers and into camp with me.

As we plodded along, the vision in my right eye became worse. Eventually, I went completely blind in that eye. To top it off, I started to hallucinate about things that weren't really there, like talking garden gnomes, for starters.

Eventually we stumbled into camp, ending Day Two. I felt ready to die. Apparently running for nine-and-a-half hours, going blind in one eye and gnome-spotting can take a lot out of a person.

My reporter friend dragged me to my tent and I passed out instantly. Then, just minutes later, I was being dragged back out of my tent by my roommates as I had started vomiting.

I spent that night in the make-shift infirmary while receiving six-and-a-half bags of IV fluid – apparently another race record.

By the time morning came around I felt substantially better and could see almost 100 percent out of my right eye again. Even better, I didn't see any more gnomes and my appetite had returned.

I called over the doctor and asked for my backpack so I could eat some breakfast. I had to regain some strength so I could get back out on the course and complete another 42 to 50 kilometers that day. I also asked that they look at my feet. I wasn't entirely certain but was pretty sure something terrible was going on. I hadn't mentioned my eyesight, nor did I want to, fearful it would mean the end of my race.

The doctor seemed nice enough but didn't share my urgency that Day Three was going to start in less than an hour. Instead, he sauntered over and told me to relax, that there was no need to rush. He informed me that I had already been disqualified.

My heart sank.

For the next few minutes, I struggled to find out why, asking the doctor for the reasoning. I'd finished both Days One and Two on my own, I hadn't received any food or water from anyone and was ready to go for Day Three. It was simple, I thought, but it turns out that when you require enough saline solution to bring back the dead, you become what is considered "High Risk."

I understood their concerns but explained that I would be running with or without their permission, so I begged them to please look at my feet and straight away. There was just no way I was going to give up like that.

The doctor reluctantly agreed to look at my feet but made me wait until after the official start of Day Three had passed to prevent me from trying to do something stupid.

I was upset and disappointed but more than anything, I was determined. Preventing me from doing something stupid would take a lot more than letting the race start without me.

19

When the doctor finally attended to my feet, he removed my socks, then sat back, shaking his head. As it turned out, during those river crossings on Day One, my feet hadn't dried as well as I thought they'd had. That, or in my drunken state during Day Two, I'd run through more water without realizing it.

He placed his hand on the bottom of my foot and slid the skin up and down a few inches. All the skin that should have stayed in place moved with his hand. Large blisters created a broken ridge through every layer of skin, from below my big toe and across to my baby toe on one foot. The other foot wasn't much better. On top of that, my feet were extremely swollen, making it look like my shoes would never fit again.

The doctor told me that he had only once tended to feet in such a terrible state. He told me about a fellow whom I had remembered reading about in the article before I signed up for the race. He was my "worst-case scenario." I recalled thinking while reading about him, 'Well, I won't be that guy!' Turns out I *was* that guy.

While I watched the last of the runners disappearing from view into the desert, the doctor told me that if the dehydration hadn't prevented me from running, my feet would have. He said there was no way I could have continued in my state. My feet were a disaster and it was time to accept the inevitable.

He was being very considerate and gentle as he realized that hearing this information wasn't easy. He had volunteered at many of these sorts of races previously and knew what it took to run in one.

I appreciated his concern but instead of accepting what he said, I took a deep breath and calmly explained that I wouldn't be giving up that easily. My feet hurt but they weren't hurting enough to stop me. Besides, pain was an old friend. It would have to keep me company while running because I was now on my own.

The doctor didn't seem impressed with my ridiculous desire to continue and refused to give me the green light to run. Still not accepting the news, I asked to speak to the race organizer. I assumed she would back down after hearing my pleas, but she didn't. My DNF became official.

I couldn't say I disagreed with her decision as I would have done the same had I been in her shoes. However, it still killed me.

With one last attempt, I explained that although I would accept the DNF, I wouldn't accept not being able to run. I hadn't put a year into training to run only 80 or 90 kilometers. I'd be giving the race my all, even if it didn't count for anything in the record books. It would count to me.

My pleas somehow worked. The race organizer agreed to let me run but not until Day Four, ensuring I took a full day to recover from what I'd put my body through on Day Two.

As much as it pained me to not run the entire event as planned, I accepted the counteroffer and spent the day trying to relax, hydrate and consume the calories I had previously skipped. I also had to come up with a solution for my shoes which now seemed about six sizes too small. The solution, as it turned out, was much easier than I would have guessed.

I had brought a pocket tool and used the knife to cut along the seam where the sole and fabric met. When I cut some of the stitches, the shoe opened up. This meant substantially less support, but I gained the much-needed space. I also loosened the laces and cut additional slits along the side of the fabric so the sides of my feet could hang out a bit. It was very makeshift, but it would work just fine, or so I hoped.

20

By the morning of Day Four I was eagerly lined up with the remaining survivors of the group, feeling pretty good, all things considered. The group of runners had dwindled substantially, many others having received DNF's due to injury, illness and at least one that had to be airlifted out. Some quit simply due to the severity of the course and how much it beat us up.

21

Each day started off with two different groups: the non-elite runners who went out first, and the elite runners who got to start an hour later. I started in the front of the first group, ecstatic to be back. Much had changed and I would forever carry a DNF, but I decided to give the course my all and aimed to enjoy it as much as possible.

My vision was back to normal and my head and stomach felt just fine. I was surprised at how well I had recovered after such a rough start. My feet hurt like hell, but I assumed the pain would dull after a few hours of running, hopefully before.

The course on Day Four started on some sort of rutted road, then led away and down into a dry riverbed consisting of fist-sized rocks for what seemed like an eternity. Every footstep had to be carefully considered to prevent the rolling of an ankle or the twisting of a knee. I worked hard to avoid both but I could feel my right foot starting to pay the price of my not being able to run flat-footed and I'm sure that the lack of support in my shoes was becoming a factor.

When I was 11 and after my last surgery, my right foot no longer had the ability to flex very much. Its range of motion is roughly 10 percent that of my left. Therefore, rather than flexing with every stone I stepped on while running, my foot was being hyper-extended.

Until that point my right foot had been acting like a superstar, or so it seemed. I don't recall having any major issues until that dry riverbed other than the issue with the loose, floppy skin on the bottom of my feet. However, after an hour or so of running in that riverbed the real pain set in. It overrode everything else I had previously experienced which made me realize it was pretty bad.

A few times I left the riverbed to run along the bank but that seemed just as bad as it was rocky as well. Plus, I couldn't see all the little pink flags I needed to watch for to avoid getting lost.

I elected to run back down in the riverbed, slowing a little, but the pain seemed to worsen. Eventually, when the metatarsal leading from my big toe finally had enough abuse, it fractured and stopped me cold.

The dry riverbed.

At first I thought I had stepped on a sharp rock so I tried to run a little more. However, I quickly realized that running would no longer be an option and walking would be hell.

Runners started passing me in trickles and eventually in groups. Some noticed my hobble and asked if I was OK. I nodded and smiled, thanked them and said everything was fine. That couldn't have been further from the truth.

22

By my calculation the next checkpoint was only a few kilometers away. I had no choice but to make it there on my own steam. I hobbled and limped wildly before realizing that walking was just as painful as running. I decided to quicken my pace, trotting over a sea of large rocks while bolts of pain shot up my foot and banged in my temples. The only thing that kept me going was sheer ignorance, stubbornness and another heaping dose of heat stroke.

After what seemed like an eternity, the course finally left that hellish riverbed and I saw the next checkpoint ahead like an oasis. I picked up the pace, doing my best to avoid limping and being pulled from the course, this time for a stress fracture.

The staff, clearly paying closer attention than I gave them credit for, sensed something had happened by my terrible running gait which was worse than normal. They hurried over and helped me to the tent, then took off my shoes. Like the doctor the morning before, they were horrified by my feet, but I assured them that they'd looked like that the day before and that it wasn't an issue.

Someone requested that I throw in the towel as I was already an official DNF, but I refused. I also refused the painkillers that someone offered. It was sometime later that I realized I may not have been in the right frame of mind, very possibly from dealing with the heat stroke. Just a few kilometers before the checkpoint I would have killed for some pain medication despite having vowed to never take it again.

Despite the strong suggestions from the race crew, I decided to continue. Somehow, I had gone from wanting to end the race just a few minutes before, to wanting to continue. It was madness but I wasn't exactly in the driver's seat considering I was dealing with heat stroke again.

I quickly put my shoes back on and explained that I had to carry on. Only 40+ kilometers to go on a fractured foot. No problem.

The staff begrudgingly topped up my water and off I went, looking to get the day over with. I hadn't even considered the fact that I still had another 140 to 160 kilometers left in the race. I didn't think like that or I may have quit right there. Instead, I only focused on the fact that I just had to get through that day. I would worry about tomorrow when I had to.

23
Although the terrain was better after that checkpoint it was far from ideal. Pain

continually shot up from my foot and overwhelmed me. I was a broken mess and had never been in so much pain in my life. I knew it was idiotic to continue but I could only think about how much I had invested in this trip and race. I also didn't want to disappoint those who knew I was there and who followed my adventures. But more than anything, I didn't want to disappoint myself.

I had some hard conversations with myself over the next handful of hours. I flip-flopped back and forth on what to do. I gave up so many times in those hours, certain I was done, only to somehow manage another few hundred meters.

I nickel and dimed myself like that until I managed roughly 26 kilometers past the last checkpoint before the pain in my foot finally got the best of me. By that point I could barely stand, let alone walk. The pain had set my entire right foot, ankle and leg on fire.

It turned out that I had completed 126 kilometers of the 250 kilometers, just a hair over half. The race had beaten me and there was no longer any point in denying it. The issue was, however, that I was nowhere near a checkpoint.

I told myself that I needed to remember the seriousness of the race and the trauma I had already put my body through, like extreme dehydration. What I had already dealt with could have led to something much worse than spending the night in the makeshift infirmary. I knew that as important as this race was to me, it wasn't worth the damage to my body.

I had started Day Four in the front of the group and finished it dead last. Even the walkers were miles ahead of me. I had been alone for hours, somewhere in the middle of the vast Gobi Desert, following little pink flags and fighting back the pain. I hadn't seen another person out there in hours as we had been crossing inhabitable parts of one of the vastest deserts on the planet.

I plunked myself onto a boulder, shoulders sunk. I was defeated in a way that I had not previously experienced. Although the pain was excruciating, my anger now overshadowed it. I was furious that my body wouldn't let me continue. Instead of considering how far my body let me go, in that moment I could only focus on how I felt it had let me down.

As the sun started getting low in the sky, fears of being left alone in the desert with no shelter and a disaster for a leg, sank in. I gave up waiting for a rescue team and started to hobble once more and in the direction of the next checkpoint. I knew that it would literally take me days to reach if no one came looking for me but I couldn't just sit there waiting. Besides, the pain was intense regardless.

I can't recall how long I dragged my broken body along, feeling absolutely helpless and more than a little concerned, before a small group of race officials found me. They were the 'sweep team' and possibly were as happy to find me as I was to see them. They treated me with kid gloves, gave me a supportive shoulder on each side and helped me hobble for another few hundred meters or so before we came to a road.

I was fortunate enough to have given up in a place where a support vehicle was able to pick me up. I rode back to camp in silence and I took in the desert from another perspective. My driver, sensing I wasn't in the mood to talk, focused on the road. I focused on my inability to finish a race for the first time in my life. I felt weak, lost and beaten.

When we finally made it back to camp, I was immediately offered a ride back to the hotel in Kashgar, a cool bed, a hot shower and real food. It was an offer too good to refuse. I wanted nothing more than to be away from this desert, the harsh conditions, the freeze-dried food I'd brought and the race that I couldn't finish.

However, I refused and stayed. I had to; there was no other option. I hadn't come to the other side of the world to completely give up. Maybe I couldn't run or even walk the rest of the course, but I could still cheer on my fellow runners, those whom the course hadn't beaten completely, and support them to the best of my ability. I felt I was still part of the team, just in a different capacity.

I won't lie to you and tell you that it was easy or that I didn't have some soul-crushing moments. Helping organize the finisher's medals at the end of Day Six was one of the hardest things I've ever done. Those medals were the nicest I've ever seen and I really wanted to take one and put it in my pocket. There were way more medals than finishers so nobody would ever have known. However, the only thing I took was a photo of the medals that I set out for the actual finishers. If I wanted to take one of those medals, I'd have to go back some day and earn it.

When the finishers started to come in on that last day, I watched the fellow from Brazil cross the finish line in his Crocs, then fall to his knees, his shoulders wrapped in the Brazilian flag, crying and clutching a photo of his child. As he kissed the ground, I fought back my own tears for him, knowing that he and the rest of the finishers had given their hearts and souls to that race. I felt what he felt. I understood, even though I would not cross that finish line.

The CNN reporter who was so completely and utterly underprepared for what she had to do, showing up the day before the race with no intention of running it, finished looking stronger than anyone else on that course. She was an absolute warrior.

The army fellow strutted in like it was no big deal. However, if one looked closely, one could see the wear and abuse on him – the same wear and abuse that hung on the faces of all the runners, including the famous ones.

As he crossed the finish line, a walker from Hong Kong whom I'd met beamed like he'd won the lottery. The Italians could be heard two kilometers back, laughing, singing, chanting and clinking their nearly empty bottles of olive oil.

The scene was overwhelming to say the least. All these amazing people whom I barely knew, coming together and taking on one of the world's toughest challenges, crossing the finish line 250-ish kilometers later, beaten but certainly not broken.

24

I spent the day after the festivities and wrap-up with the fellow from Brazil and who had run in the Crocs. Turns out he had been sponsored ever since he ran around the entirety of Brazil non-stop. Now he runs the world in Crocs and gets paid to do so.

I spent the following day with one of the Italians, further exploring Kashgar. Turns out he worked for a chocolatier that had asked him to invent a new chocolate for the company. He invented a very famous, well known chocolate treat found around the world. After that impressive invention, he retired by opening a bookstore in Italy and running crazy races.

Everyone I met had an amazing story to tell, yet everyone was extremely humble and gracious. Some had beat cancer before coming to the Gobi Desert, others had beat serious addictions. Some were there to drastically change or reboot their lives, others to push themselves to new limits.

We all came from different walks of life and different parts of the world. We came together to run, walk and share in an event that taught us all something special about what we were really capable of. We realized that the Gobi March wasn't just a physical event but a spiritual, emotional and psychological battle and that running was only a small part of it. We came together and conquered our fears. We laughed and joked. We shared, we overcame and eventually we went our separate ways, every one of us a hero.

The one that got away.

Chapter 12 – Losing It

I returned to Canada feeling surprisingly good considering I had dedicated so much time and training to an event that ended up being my first DNF. Did Not Finish is not something a runner wants to see written next to their name. However, instead of wasting my time sulking, I wore it well and vowed to use it to make myself a better runner. Besides, I had honestly considered the entire experience to be a positive lesson as I'd learned a lot about what I was truly capable of doing. It had opened my mind to other possibilities. Previously, I had thought that running a marathon under my circumstances would be an incredible feat. However, I came to realize that I hadn't even been scratching the surface of what was truly incredible. That mountain goes much higher, and I realized it was only a matter of being able to dream it, believe in oneself, then take steps in that direction.

2
During the two days it took me to travel back to Canada, I started formulating another goal.

Before training for the Gobi March, I had assumed that running a marathon a day for multiple days was not possible. Of course, I quickly learned that not only was it possible, but it was possible for me as well. OK, perhaps it wasn't great for the body, but neither was the way I was living my life prior to running.

I started wondering what I was really capable of doing. I thought back to my early days of running as far as I could in one direction. I loved those simple days, running straight from "Point A" to "Point Wherever I Could Manage." I then started thinking about what it would be like to travel somewhere new and, well, do the same but over multiple days. I dreamed of basically landing somewhere exciting, running straight out of the airport and seeing how far I could go in a week, or perhaps, a month.

That simple idea quickly evolved into something pretty exciting to me. I started to scratch down ideas while on my flight back from China. I realized, of course, that I would have to wait for my foot to heal as well as look into options to prevent that from happening again. However, the seed of an idea had been planted and fertilized and was already starting to sprout.

3

I made it back to Edmonton, happy to be home and excited about my next adventure. Life seemed to be on the up-and-up. My health was decent, my business was growing and I had something huge to look forward to with my running. Life couldn't have been any better, or so it seemed. However, it was early 2008 and the impending housing crash in the US was already underway. I had no idea what was coming or that it would affect my business in the way it did. I was just months from experiencing the greatest financial and personal disasters of my life.

4

When I had traveled to China, I had an office in a prominent part of Edmonton, a business partner and staff. We were growing nicely. I felt proud of my business, especially after the risks I'd taken by starting it rather than falling back into another high-paying retail management position.

Then, as the spring of 2008 turned to summer, I started seeing the fragility of my business. I owned a Canadian business that held US Dollar contracts with major running events around the world and I only had the ability to collect Canadian Dollars from my clients. To deal with the slight currency fluctuations I had been building a small exchange buffer into all my travel packages but was far from ready for the 26% dive our Dollar would take in roughly

11 months. At the time I had roughly USD 300,000 in signed contracts. This meant that, assuming I could still sell all my travel packages, I would lose around USD 78,000. That's a big number for a new company that wasn't making large profits. Looking back, I would have been very happy if that was all I would eventually lose. Unfortunately, the amount I lost skyrocketed to over six figures as Canadians were no longer comfortable spending the extra 26% to go on a trip and I couldn't sell all of the product I had pre-purchased.

In the span of a few weeks, I had to let my staff go, I lost my office and had to sell all my personal possessions again − including my vehicle, furniture and computer equipment − just to keep up with the minimums on my credit cards. To make matters worse, the entire company had been started and maintained on my personal credit. That being the case, I had spent all my personal savings and maxed out all my credit cards and line of credit to keep things hobbling along. I went from being completely debt-free and having a perfect credit rating to sitting on the floor in my apartment and missing meals, knowing I was in my final month of having a roof over my head.

At the same time, I had a falling out with my business partner whom I had brought on after the second year. It was either buy him out or close the business entirely. It was an extremely risky move, but I don't give up easily. Besides, I was stubborn enough to assume that eventually I could turn things around. More importantly, I had a group of 150 clients who were due to depart on a marathon tour with me a few months later; I couldn't simply default on them.

In 2001, when I ran my first marathon, the company I went through had collected my payment, then gone under before paying for the components of my trip. There was no way I was going to do that to my clients. I was hell bent on making all the necessary payments and then going personally bankrupt if necessary. *Whatever it takes*, I thought. I wouldn't be able to live with myself had I abandoned the ship before it was already sunk.

5

Although the Dream Travel ship hadn't sunk, I recall running the numbers after tapping into the more than $130,000 in credit I had at the time. It looked like I was going to scrape through with literally a couple hundred dollars of credit left. That was assuming I could start to sell again.

During these extremely stressful months, my friend Clinton had found a gig house-sitting in Costa Rica for seven weeks. He suggested that I come down and get away from the stress so that I could focus solely on reviving my business. I thought it beyond crazy and irresponsible but at the same time, I knew I was two weeks away from being homeless. Plus, Clinton had built a company into a million-dollar business from scratch in about a year's time, so he always had great advice and tips on how to improve my business. The only issue was that I had enough space on my remaining credit card for either a flight or another month of moving around payments. There was no choice to be made; I declined his offer.

Although my stress levels were at an all-time high, I kept my head up and somehow felt that I could turn things around. I'm sure anyone who really knew how deep I was in the hole, in all aspects, would have thought me the biggest fool for thinking that way. However, I've always believed that things have a way of working themselves out.

6

I remember sitting in my apartment, which then stood absolutely bare, just two bags beside me containing some clothes, my running gear and a few books. Absolutely everything else had either been sold or given to charity. It was my final day in my apartment, my home for the previous seven years, and I was waiting around for the mailman to come one last time. I had no plan at all, nowhere to go, yet I never considered calling family or friends for help. I would give up only when that was the absolutely last option. That said, the clock had basically run out and I just hadn't noticed.

7

At 1PM, when I was sure the mailman had come, I headed down to the front lobby to collect my mail for the last time.

Thinking back, I'm unsure how I held my composure so well. I had put all of my eggs into that one basket: my business. And even though I had something to fall back on - my retail management experience - I hadn't even considered applying for a job. I was all in with my company, but I was also literally flat broke and with nowhere to go. That said, being homeless had always been somewhat of a concern of mine but I suppose in the back of my mind, I felt that I could eventually find a friend's sofa to crash on until I sorted out my life.

Perhaps the fear of being homeless had first taken hold when I gave up my high-paying career and started pursuing a life that I enjoyed rather than one that paid well. And perhaps once I walked out the front door of my apartment that day I would have started to freak out, realizing I'd either have to find a dry, warm corner in which to sleep or admit that I made a mistake by leaving the illusion of normality and following my dreams. If the latter were the case, I'd need to then start calling friends for a place to crash. I dreaded the thought of having to admit defeat or worse, asking for help.

As fate would have it, I wouldn't have to worry about making those desperate phone calls. All I had to do was open my mailbox that final time. Amongst the multiple Final Notice letters and credit card bills was a letter from the estate of my grandmother.

8

My grandmother had died a month or so before I found myself going through my mail that day. Sadly, I didn't know either of my paternal grandparents well. Or to be honest, I really didn't know them at all, perhaps seeing them only a handful of times in my entire life. When my father died, we moved to another province and slowly lost touch. And since my father died when I was just a toddler, I grew up without them being around and then that just became the norm.

It was unfortunate and I would love to share some better reasons as to why, but they would only amount to a mountain of precariously stacked excuses.

Despite not knowing my paternal grandparents as a child, I did try to get to know them and that side of the family a little better as an adult, but by then it was too late.

I had gone to visit them just a couple of times when my grandfather fell ill and died shortly after. I had managed to see him just hours prior to his passing, and then was present for his funeral. Sadly, however, I didn't have enough money to fly out and attend my grandmother's funeral. It was either be present for her funeral or make a required minimum payment on a business credit card.

Even though I knew very little about them, I did know that they had been the poorest people in my family, which would have been a difficult feat. That said, I most certainly wasn't expecting any money. Instead, I assumed it would be a letter from her, maybe something she wrote when she was ill.

Standing there in the lobby, my two duffle bags with what was left of my possessions at my feet, I stared at the envelope from my grandmother's estate feeling bewildered.

Inside was a cheque for $2,000.

9
I was stunned. It was waiting in my mailbox on

what could have been the worst day of my life. Had I not waited for my mail that day, I honestly have no idea what would have happened to myself or my company. Perhaps I would have given up and gone back into retail, finding work in some big-box store in Edmonton, dreaming of the life that I always wanted instead of actually living it.

What I do know, looking back now, is that the cheque altered my life in a truly staggering way.

I called Clinton, told him to prepare a room and said that I would be on the next flight to Costa Rica.

10

The plan was to go for ten days, rebuild my business, then come back to Canada and sort things out. That was it. Nothing else. No housing plans, no job plans. Just focus solely on the business and assume it will all work out.

Of course, that's not how it happened. How it did go down, however, wasn't something I could ever have expected.

My first two days in Costa Rica were very hard and I hated being there. I couldn't stand the heat, the bugs and the fact that I didn't know Spanish. By the third day, however, something happened: I started to let go. I had realized that I was simply stressed and rightfully so. I had been angry and was taking it out on my new surroundings. Instead of appreciating the beauty of where I was or even the beach, I was focused on despair.

On the third day, I woke up early to the sound of the surf crashing on the beach. We were staying just 100 meters from an incredible stretch of beach in a little town called Uvita. It was early and Clinton had still been asleep, so I threw on my running shoes and headed down for a quick run.

The beach stretched about 5KM and was absolutely deserted at that early hour. The sun was just rising and made for a picturesque setting right out of a movie.

Something shifted in me while running along that beach. I let go of the rest of the anger and the fear and I remembered something I always told others, that everything eventually works out in the end. I focused on that thought and enjoyed the run, the feeling of the cool breeze coming off the ocean, the beach lined with palm trees and the sounds of the Howler Monkey's off in the distance.

That run was absolutely beautiful and I decided that I would start every morning like that for the rest of my trip. Not just for the exercise, but for the release.

With each additional day that passed on that trip, I worked on my business plan and fell more and more in love with that little corner of Costa Rica. I enjoyed myself so much that by the end of the trip I knew that I would one day call Costa Rica home.

One day.

I finished my ten-day stint with Clinton, went back to Canada eager to put my new business plan into place. The only issue was, I still had nowhere to live. Instead of looking for a sofa to crash on, I decided there and then that living in Costa Rica 'one day' needed to happen immediately.

Within two weeks of landing back in Canada, I had flown back to Costa Rica and was officially living there. The $2,000 my grandmother had left me paid for my flights, a furnished house for six months on the beach, all my food and had left me with just enough to bounce some more payments around on my credit cards to keep the bank at arms' length.

I spent those six months reinventing my business, turning it around completely and taking me from my worst year ever in 2008 to my best year ever in 2009 and by far.

I had to give up my lifestyle, friends and family and was living in a foreign land, not knowing the language or anyone else as Clinton had already left, but I had saved my business.

Those six months slowly morphed into three years of living in Costa Rica even though I had paid off half of my debt within the first year and the balance the following. I couldn't see any real reason to return to Canada when I was able to successfully run my business from abroad, and, better than ever.

The beach

My idea of paradise

PART IV

Setbacks and Resets

PARIS, FRANCE 2013

The sun slowly rises over the River Seine, illuminating the Eiffel Tower. It takes my breath away. I'm sitting alone on the riverbank, listening to the early morning birds, mesmerized by the sight. It's nothing short of intoxicating. Although it's a sight I've seen many times, it never fails to captivate me when I'm here.

The idea of running the world still excites me on a level that's hard to describe. I simply can't imagine a life without it, especially here in Paris. There's nothing quite like running on cobblestone-lined streets early in the mornings while I still have the city mostly to myself.

Although I'm ecstatic to be back in this incredible city, I'm certain that this time my experience will be very different. I'm about to be very ill and I know it as my body is giving me all the signs. My energy levels are extremely low, I'm dealing with considerably more inflammation than normal and I can't stop sweating.

2
Despite heading out for an early morning run, I

don't think I managed 500 meters before I have to sit, utterly exhausted. I want to believe it's because Paris in the summer can be very hot, and this year it seems stifling, but honestly, I know better. My body's trying to talk to me but I'm doing my best to ignore it. I don't want to ruin this trip but I'm all but certain that my body is   about   to   revolt.

I'm halfway through a six year, non-stop trip around the world with my girlfriend. We typically spend only a few weeks – sometimes only a handful of days – in each country before moving on. I keep making mental notes to slow down a little, spend more time in each place and create more of a routine.

Routines are important, especially for my body. I need a routine to stay healthy as I've discovered that the four triggers of Crohn's disease for me are sugar, alcohol, stress and lack of sleep. When you live out of a bag and constantly eat in restaurants, those are all difficult to avoid – or so I've chosen to believe.

Running can allow some of the diet to slide a little, but my body is always quick to tell me when I've done – or consumed – something I should not have. Honestly, I'm appreciative as it keeps me in line. Mostly. Although if I'm being honest with myself, the past few years I've been enjoying the freedom of travel, eating out and over-indulging a little too much. Now it has caught up with me.

I want to blame it on the travel, different foods and stress of constantly changing time zones. But this isn't my first rodeo and I've learned to adapt nicely while on the road. Or so I thought. Besides, I know how to eat right, I know what my body needs. However, I've been in 'celebration' mode far too long and my body had been begging me for a reset. Since I ignored it for as long as I have, it's decided to take control.

3

My girlfriend and I both love Paris so I thought we would start that new routine of moving around a little slower here, spending at least a month in the city, then heading back to Spain and eventually down to Morocco again before flying to New York for the 2013 New York City Marathon. We would give ourselves just over four months to get there.

My training had been going well and I had even convinced my non-runner girlfriend to come out for a few runs with me. However, in the past week I haven't had the energy to run. At first I assumed my energy would return. Then I started to realize that it was tied to Crohn's disease and that I might be sidelined for a while longer. I didn't share my thoughts or concerns with my girlfriend in the hopes that I was wrong or that my situation would magically improve. However, my mind kept returning to when we were in Thailand, just a year or so previously, where I felt myself getting sick just before the discovery of a tumor in my rectum.

4

I finish watching the sun rise before I pick myself up and head back to the hotel. The only thing I want now is a quick shower, then to get back into bed. However, we're in Paris and I know that my girlfriend is excited to get out and wander the city. It's one of her favorite cities and I don't want to let her down.

Despite being absolutely wiped, I take my girlfriend to the Eiffel Tower. Usually I make her walk everywhere with me but today I call a taxi. Now she knows something's up.

I try to deny it but she can see that sitting in the back of the taxi causes me substantial pain even though I was fine just an hour earlier while sitting on the hard ground. It never ceases to amaze me how fast the abscesses come on.

We spend just enough time at the Eiffel Tower to take a couple of pictures before she tells me we're going back to the hotel. She wants to inspect me and we both know better than to do that in public, especially considering where this particular abscess is growing.

For the past two decades I've had an abscess site high on my backside, thanks to Crohn's and the subsequent holes in my intestines. It's not the most romantic place to show your girlfriend but she never complains and always tends to it when necessary by lancing and draining it. As bad as it sounds, it works quite well and within minutes of its draining, I typically feel better.

Today, however, I have a new abscess and it's in a very different location, behind my testicles. This makes it impossible to sit and painful to even lay down.

It's been perhaps three hours since I was sitting on the steps, looking at the Eiffel Tower. I was ill but the abscess hadn't yet formed, at least not to the point that I could feel it. Now I'm lying in bed, sweating profusely and in substantial pain. The location makes it very dangerous to lance as the bacteria could easily spread the infection to neighboring areas of my body – and that would not be good. I also know that if I wait much longer, the abscess could grow to be larger than my fist, which is something I've experienced more than once. It's extremely dangerous and my girlfriend decides to look for a hospital that's close by.

5

Another side effect of a chronic disease is that you don't qualify for full travel insurance. It's a thought that briefly enters my mind while I'm lying across the backseat of a taxi on the way to the hospital that my girlfriend found. I can't imagine that an emergency procedure, even day surgery, would be cheap in this city.

I push away the thought as best as I can as I have no alternative.

6

After a nurse quickly glances at my undercarriage, I'm quickly admitted for emergency surgery. I want to know exactly what's going on so that I can fill my girlfriend in and mentally prepare myself, but so far, I hear only French. My doctor sees that I don't understand and apologizes in broken English, explaining that he speaks only French and Spanish. I apologize in Spanish for not being able to speak French, and that Spanish would do just fine. It's a very lucky break on a day that could potentially be very damaging not only to my body but also my checkbook.

I'm laid out on my stomach, buttocks up and out for all to see. After a few moments of excruciating poking and prodding, the doctor asks me how many weeks my abscess has been growing and why I left it so long. I try to explain that it literally came on just a few hours before, but he doesn't believe it. He claims that he has never seen an abscess so large nor one that came on so fast. I jokingly tell him that I do nothing half-assed. It didn't translate well so I chuckle to myself while praying for the morphine to kick in.

7

The surgeon performed the surgery and I spent the night in the hospital, my girlfriend at my side all night in a chair. Instead of thinking about my health and being grateful for the company, I'm adding up all the individual charges I'll have to deal with in the morning.

When that time finally comes and I'm cleared by my new Spanish-speaking French doctor friend, he apologizes once more, this time for the bill. He understands that I'm not covered and the look on his face re-enforces my fear. It's going to be disastrous. I start wondering what would have happened if my girlfriend had attempted to drain it herself. I decide to ask him for his professional opinion about that and he violently shakes his head. I want to explain to him that although I own a business and travel the world, I'm not rich. In fact, I'm far from it. It's just considerably less expensive to live a life like I have than to lead a normal life in Canada.

He starts counting off the very potential complications of trying to deal with such a large abscess that's on the inside of my body, not the outside. It was so large that it only looked to be external.

He solemnly hands me the bill. I immediately scan the bottom for the total but all I can see is 1,800 Euros. Surely that's only for the anesthesiologist or maybe his own fees, I ask. He seems confused but assures me that the total bill comes to 1,800, or roughly CAD 2,500.

We leave the hospital, my girlfriend depressed by the amount I just spent and me ready to party hard with some fresh croissants and strawberry jam. Being from Costa Rica and not ever having needed surgery, she can't understand how it could have been so expensive. I, on the other hand, know full well that it could have been as much as four or five times that amount and am extremely grateful. That said, I'd be more grateful with a bag of warm croissants. However, she's telling me that I have to watch what I eat, as if that isn't obvious. Apparently, it isn't, and I deem it necessary to indulge, at least for the day. Tomorrow, I think, I'll start taking better care of my body.

8

Post-abscess drainage and taking care of my body on that sort of scale means either: 1) returning to the hospital twice a day for at least two weeks to have a nurse pull a few meters of packing material out of the freshly drained cavity via a small hole the surgeon left open, clean the inside of the wound with saline solution, then re-pack it with fresh packing or 2) have my girlfriend do that for me.

My girlfriend graciously agrees to do the work, saving us an untold amount of money and allowing me to openly complain about the pain and to squirm while she and her thick fingers poke gauze into my new hole on a regular basis. She puts up with the work and my whining like a trooper.

Although we don't get around to all our favorite places in Paris, the trip is far from ruined. We're both grateful things weren't worse.

We postpone Spain and Morocco and instead buy a couple of tickets to Canada to see my specialist there. Although I'm confident that I'll recover, it's time that I find a way to prevent future abscesses as I'm now experiencing one every couple of months. My body had been begging me for change and I was finally going to oblige.

Painfully beautiful

Chapter 13 – The Turn Around

Being forced to leave Canada in 2008, as it felt at the time, turned out to be an incredible gift. I fell in love with Costa Rica, the way of life, the beaches and people, the food and weather. Even though I had turned my business around in record time and could have returned to Canada after those first six months, I realized that I could run my business just as efficiently from paradise as I could from Edmonton. Plus, I would never have to worry about putting on winter clothes or running on snow and ice.

As those six months in Costa Rica turned into years, and while my business continued to grow and prosper, I learned a new language and appreciation for living a minimalist lifestyle, which I've continued to stick with. I learned to save even more money, in case I experienced another economic crisis which is good as that major financial setback was only the first of four, each being just as disastrous or substantially worse.

2

The bane of many a great small business owners is the idea that by being our own bosses, we'll work less, maybe get rich, but ultimately, create more freedom to focus on what's most important to us in life. However, the truth is that most of us tend to get trapped by the ridiculous number of hours required to keep our businesses alive. It takes its toll. Roughly 80 percent of small businesses fail within the first three years, 90 percent within five and 99 percent within 10.

Not only did I want to avoid losing my business, but I also didn't want to fall into that hole of working more and enjoying life less. However, I knew that the odds were greatly stacked against me as I'd previously experienced when I barely scraped by with the money my grandmother had left me. I had to find a way to focus on my business while maintaining a realistic balance, allowing me to live my life, run and still enjoy what I did. I was determined to find the uncommon balance of work and pleasure that few seemed to experience, even if it meant stunting my own business growth. I refused to be a statistic, to grow tired of a business I loved or to lose sight of why I had initially started the company. I started my company so that I could travel the world and run; therefore, the solution was easy. It was time to start traveling, this time for real.

3
It was then, during one of the worst economic

downturns, that I decided to once again put together a trip to Tanzania, Africa. I knew that regardless of the economy, those who had money would always have money. If I built and priced the package well, people would buy it.

I had been on this particular trip a few times by then and it was definitely one of my favorites. I was looking forward to returning and decided to invite my girlfriend, who by then, had never left Costa Rica, nor even been on an airplane. She happily agreed.

I don't think she had barely responded when I asked her what she thought about extending the trip by a few weeks. I argued my point that because we were flying across the world, I thought we could make it a little more worthwhile. When she agreed so easily the second time, I started considering the idea that we could build in a few other stops.

In the end I purchased two one-way tickets to Tanzania as we weren't sure from where we would fly back. Our expected four- to five-week trip turned into our multi-year, nonstop journey around the world.

4

I was finally living the life I'd always wanted – or almost. We were traveling and seeing some of the most exciting places on the planet.

However, I wasn't running nearly as much as I wanted. My health had improved drastically while I lived in Costa Rica as I was eating clean, healthy food. However, traveling meant eating in restaurants constantly as well as changing types and sources of food. We hopped from country to country, spending a maximum of two weeks per place but typically less. I loved it, but my stomach hated it. I started developing record numbers of abscesses, some leading to emergency surgeries while abroad like the one in Paris.

I dealt with constant and extreme inflammation that sometimes made me look like I weighed 30 to 40 pounds more than I did, and for weeks or months at a time. Running became extremely difficult and less of a priority. My girth and puffiness embarrassed me, yet controlling it meant making some hard choices – ones that I wasn't ready to make.

It's not common to consider the upside of having a chronic condition like Crohn's disease. However, if asked, I would quickly say that it keeps me in control, giving me constant reminders to take better care of myself. I've grown to appreciate that about what I have as you can't fight a disease like Crohn's by eating and drinking whatever you want, whenever you want. That said, my diet was starting to take a backseat to my lifestyle once again.

5

We had made our way to Southeast Asia, narrowing in on our 54th straight month of travel when I started feeling a little better. I began running again and was grateful for the energy and ability, especially after having taken such a hiatus. I became more optimistic that I was turning my health around. However, this was very short-lived. It was simply the calm before the storm.

I may have been running for a couple of weeks (short, easy five-kilometer jogs at best), but I noted that they were becoming more and more difficult to get through. At first I thought it was because of the extreme heat and humidity of Thailand, or because of the fact that I was a bit older by then or because of the extra pounds I was packing. Regardless, I dismissed it for a while, focusing on getting out as much as I could. I certainly felt better in general than I previously had, so I assumed it was something else, not related to Crohn's.

We made our way to Chiang Mai in the northern part of Thailand where the weather was much more agreeable. However, I found my runs to be harder, not easier. During my last run there, along a country road on the cusp of the Thai jungle, I was forced to cut my run short after only two kilometers. I felt absolutely exhausted. I started walking, wondering why I felt as if I had just run a marathon. The weather felt considerably cooler compared to the heat of the islands, yet I was sweating buckets and desperately wanted to sit.

I stopped long enough to take a breather, then sauntered back in the direction of my hotel, defeated. A few moments later, I felt something warm running down the back of one leg. At first I assumed it was sweat, yet I somehow knew better. I slowly reached back, wiped at my leg with a shaking hand, then looked to see if it was what I thought it might be. It was, and I was terrified.

6

I hate to think that I've spent any time considering the fact that cancer is a real risk for someone like me. However, the truth is, although I haven't spent a lot of time thinking about it over the years, the thought has crossed my mind, and maybe more than it should have. Not only am I at a higher risk due to Crohn's, but my father and both grandfathers died of cancer and two of them had taken very good care of themselves. And, over the years my doctors have always casually reminded me that I'm prone to tumors and hence, require additional and frequent tests.

All these thoughts came rushing into my head as I held my hand in front of my face while I looked at the blood on my fingers.

7

Shooting rectal pain wasn't uncommon for me but it had become more common during the last few months of travel. I hadn't told my girlfriend about the pain. I tried to forget it myself, as hard as that was some days. Now, however, there was no more hiding. The source of the pain was clear.

Needless to say, our years-long trip was finally over. We flew to Canada a couple of days later.

8

We weren't back in Canada more than 48 hours before my specialist had me lying on a metal gurney while he performed a sigmoidoscopy. Sigmoids are similar to colonoscopies, but the long, cable-like devices, which are rectally administered, have a few upgrades like the ability to blow air, water and take biopsies. In addition, patients are usually awake during the entire procedure. It's one of my least favorite procedures but at least it only lasts 10 to 15 minutes. That is, of course, unless the doctor finds something.

I was lying on my side in the operating theatre while my doctor did his thing behind me. We were both watching the large TV monitor directly in front of me as the snake-like camera worked its way through me. My doctor gave me the play by play, explaining what we were both seeing on the screen. He had been rooting around in there for less than three minutes when the tumor came into view, taking up way too much of the screen in front of me.

As much as I appreciated my doctor, he didn't mince words or hold back. He made it clear that this was the cause of the blood loss and that he had been, in fact, expecting to find it. He said that it may very well be cancer. He spent the next few minutes tearing it out using the micro-sized robotic, hand-like gadget that was front-mounted to the device inside me. I watched in horror, unable to breathe. A deep-seated fear seemed to be coming true and I had a front-row seat and a large plasma TV to show me everything in graphic, gory detail.

9

I like to think I'm a fairly patient person, but the necessity of waiting for results made for a very difficult handful of days. It seemed that my entire life was on hold while I waited to find out what was in that terrifying lump inside my colon.

I started to realize that the three things I cared about most – running, traveling and my business – may all have been coming to a quick end. No way was I going to continue working if I had cancer, but I also didn't want to be in Canada while going through treatment. I wanted to pack up, get out of town, and lose myself in Europe, Africa or Asia. Anywhere, just to put this all behind me and continue on with my life.

Clearly, I wasn't being mature about it. That was just my way of dealing with the situation. Avoidance, or something along those lines.

When the call finally came, my doctor told me that the lump he had removed was precancerous. I didn't know precisely what that meant, but he assured me that other than doing a few follow-up tests over the following months, followed by yearly exams, I should be fine. Fine, assuming it didn't come back.

He also told me that he was able to remove the entire lump, or so he felt. However, he made it clear that he was confident, but not certain.

When I returned some months later to have a follow-up scope, there was no sign of the tumor. Everything looked squeaky clean as he had in fact removed everything.

10

I felt like a free man again. Free to travel, free to run and free to live my life, but with a few dietary changes coming down the pipe, so to speak. I could live with that. Besides, I knew that I had been abusing my body with too much sugar, alcohol and bad food in general once again. I vowed to make some real changes and to not be a statistic, like the one stating that 99 percent of people given a real health scare don't actually change their habits. That would not be me.

The results had been very freeing. I started to think that it was time to focus on completing other important things in my life, like pulling my "dream run" out of the planning stages and turning it into a reality. Despite feeling that I was living a charmed life, I was still avoiding some things that were important to me like that run.

For instance, since returning home from the Gobi March, I'd had the crazy idea of going to a country where I hadn't previously visited and simply running as far as I could in 30 days. The idea had changed over time, but in the end, I decided to go to Ireland and run 32 kilometers per day for 30 consecutive days. On Day 31, I would run the Dublin Marathon. In total, my goal was to run 1,000 kilometers through the beautiful Irish countryside in one month.

I'd set the plan in my head for some time, yet I hadn't pulled the trigger. Now, I decided that to celebrate being healthy, I would make it happen.

The very next day I purchased our flights to Ireland.

11

Before traveling to Ireland we returned to Costa Rica where my sole goal was to train my butt off for six months and get myself up to comfortably running a half marathon a day. I rented a cheap, cockroach-infested hotel beside Central America's largest urban park and trained religiously. I also focused on eating healthy, including cutting out sugar and alcohol. Before I knew it, I was looking slim and trim. I'd never felt better in my life.

I knew it was a crazy goal, but I honestly felt ready to take it on, even more so than the Gobi March. My run through Ireland would be at my own pace and hence there would be no pressure. I could run on my schedule, plotting my course day-by-day. My girlfriend, who wanted to bike beside me, would help by carrying food and water and providing moral support on what would be my biggest challenge yet. I could take my time, walk if necessary and just enjoy the process. I'd have from sun up to sun down to run and the evenings to work. It seemed perfect.

12

My training had gone incredibly well. I had managed to work up to running back-to-back half marathons every day for a week with hardly any pain in my foot and leg. Plus, I had been training in the heat and humidity of Costa Rica which would be much more uncomfortable than the temperate climate of Ireland. Plus, I had pushed myself in Costa Rica and was turning out decent half marathon times every day, whereas in Ireland I would slow it down and enjoy each day at a jogging pace. I felt more than ready to tackle the challenge and was completely confident I would complete it as planned.

13

By the time we landed in Dublin, the idea of running like this had been a dream of mine for four or five years. It was the biggest goal I could dream up that I thought was doable. I knew that such an experience would change my life. I put my heart and soul into following that dream and it was unbelievable to land in Ireland!

14

In Howth, just outside Dublin, we spent the first few nights with an old friend whom I'd met during my 10-year job stint in Edmonton. My goal was to get over the jetlag and, of course, raise a few pints and fatten up with fish and chips. I would need the energy, after all.

15

The morning to start finally arrived. My girlfriend had her bike and gear ready and I was chomping at the bit to get started. My friend saw us off, wishing us luck and I started running towards Dublin. The plan was to run to the far west side of the city, finish the 32 kilometers and then find a cheap hotel.

Running in Ireland felt great, especially due to the weather, which was much cooler than I was used to in Costa Rica. We ran out of Howth, past the homes of some of the U2 band members and the bar where they hung out, and towards the capital of Ireland.

We had made it through the center of Dublin and were closing in on 22 kilometers when my girlfriend asked me to stop so that she could take photos of me. She had decided that she should document my epic run and that Phoenix Park, which we'd reached when she asked me to stop, would make for a nice backdrop.

I left the roadway and took a few steps onto the grass. Then I turned to face her and heard a loud pop. I fell to the ground, clutching my left knee.

16

I lay on the ground, looking dumbfounded at the rock that I had stepped on wrong. At first, I thought that maybe I had just twisted my knee a little and tried to walk it off. Then I realized it was much worse. I knew that my dream had just come to an end. Almost five years of dreaming, six months of dedicated and intense training and thousands of dollars – all gone in one terrible moment. I had run roughly 22 of a planned 1,000 kilometers. The pain was terrible but more than anything, I was angry. Extremely angry.

I rode the bike to the far side of the park, using my good leg to slowly push myself along while my girlfriend walked quietly beside me. She knew how much this run had meant to me and somehow felt it was her fault. I assured her it wasn't, it was just incredibly bad luck. I had never twisted a knee, ankle or anything in my life despite the fact that I'd run on snow and ice for countless winters in Edmonton.

We found a hotel and I put ice on my knee, hoping that by the next day I would be good enough to run again. In the end, we stayed in that hotel for five nights. Each morning I tried to put more weight on my knee and each morning realizing that there was just no way. I was done. There would be no more running for the foreseeable future. I gave up my dream and did my best to put it behind me.

17

Fortunately, I had shared my idea of running across Ireland with only a very small group of people. I figured most wouldn't understand or care. And honestly, I wanted to keep it to myself. That turned out to be a good thing, as having to explain what happened to a lot of people would have been very difficult.

One of the people I had shared it with, however, had chosen to come to Ireland with his wife and kids to run the Dublin Marathon as his first marathon, and to support me on what was supposed to be my final day of running in Ireland.

I was shocked and honored that they would spend that much time and money to go all the way to Ireland when he could have chosen any number of marathons close to where they lived.

Now, lying in a hotel room, nursing my knee and sulking about what could have been, I realized that they were coming, and that Barry would be running Dublin as his first marathon. There was no way I could let him down. I vowed to run the marathon, which was just a little over three weeks later.

18

Now that I couldn't complete my goal I couldn't stand to be in Ireland. I wanted to leave but knew that I had to come back for the marathon.

After a quick search I found cheap flights to Japan and we flew out the next day. I figured I'd rather limp around Japan than Ireland but more than anything, I felt that it wouldn't sting as much being somewhere other than where I had planned to run. Besides, I knew that I would have to one day go back and re-attempt my dream run.

I had always wanted to visit Japan but not under those circumstances. Besides, walking was very painful at first so it wasn't like I could do much. It had crossed my mind to see a doctor, of course, but every day it got a little better, or so I told myself.

We did our best to enjoy ourselves in Japan, then headed back to Ireland a handful of days prior to the race.

19

A few days before the marathon, I met with

Barry, Karen and their wonderful kids in Dublin. They were aware of my little accident and I let on that I was fine. The truth was, I was far from fine. My knee still really hurt but I was going to run the marathon if it killed me. Of course, that was arrogant and ridiculous, but I knew how much training Barry had put in. I didn't want to let him down.

It started off better than I could have imagined, but by the time I managed maybe eight or nine kilometers, my knee really started acting up. By halfway I was hobbling and by 35 kilometers I was in extreme pain. I should have stopped but I couldn't. I did the foolish thing and pushed on.

My girlfriend had been waiting at various points along the course, cheering us on. She watched me deteriorate and knew that I was struggling. By the time I was on the home stretch, the finish line five or six blocks away, I felt like I was almost the only one left on the course. I had been losing time since the fifth kilometer and just focused on finishing. I was elated to see the finish line, even though it still looked kilometers away.

I remember wanting to walk off that course more times than I could count, but I kept pushing on and focusing my energy on getting across the finish line.

I was a bit lost in my thoughts when I caught sight of a spectator standing in the middle of the course. I remember wondering who would do that and why so close to the finish line. Then I realized that the spectator was no longer standing but running directly towards me. My girlfriend flung herself into my arms, crying and almost knocking us both to the ground. She sobbed that she was proud of me and it broke my heart. She helped me hobble across the finish line to the cheers of the spectators, squeezing me so tightly I almost forgot how much my knee hurt.

20

In the end, I ran a total of 63 kilometers out of the planned 1,000 kilometers. Somehow, I was OK with it. In the 30 days between hurting my knee and crossing the Dublin Marathon's finish line, I'd had enough time to deal with the loss of that dream. I've always believed that everything happens for a reason and I had no doubt that there was a good reason why I'd been unable to complete that goal. The fact that I didn't know the reason didn't matter. I simply trusted that it wasn't meant to be – or at least, it wasn't meant to be then and there. No one said I couldn't attempt it again, in another time and place.

Chapter 14 – Pain in My Backside

After the Dublin Marathon we returned to Costa Rica to sort out what was next. We assumed that we would travel more but we wanted to get a little rest while planning the next months or years of travel.

I had assumed that my health was on the rebound as I hadn't experienced any problems while training nor while in Ireland, but of course that had been only a handful of months. As it turned out, the discovery of the tumor was simply the start of another string of health setbacks that would plague me for the next five years. I would barely rebound from one abscess and all that accompanied it, then have a handful of good months during which I could resume training before another started to form, slowly sucking the energy from my body and killing both my desire and ability to run.

It was a vicious cycle that ended each time with a night or two in the hospital, surgery and typically a reprimand from a doctor for not having gone to a hospital sooner.

Just like before and due to the extreme size of most of the abscesses, the doctors assumed that they'd been growing for weeks at a minimum and that I had simply put off dealing with them. I explained that although I'd start feeling weak as early as three or four days prior, I'd never let 36 hours pass from the time I noticed the abscess until the time I crawled into the hospital.

After each surgery, a nurse would go through the unpacking and repacking procedure of my wound with my girlfriend so that she could do it for me, saving me daily trips to the hospital.

This packing/repacking process with the gauze was so painful that it made the time I had an abscess drainage, without being sedated, seem like child's play.

The healing, gauze removal and repacking process normally took as much as three or four weeks, depending on the size of the abscess. Fortunately, each day was a little less painful than the previous one and each surgery seemed a little easier and less painful. I'm fairly certain that either I'm growing accustomed to the pain or that the nerves in my nether regions are dying off from the constant surgeries and punishment from the almost always-present abscesses.

To date, I've had these procedures done in Costa Rica, France, Azerbaijan and more times than I can count in Canada. Now the most painful part of the process isn't the packing of the wound but the paying of the hospital bills while abroad as I'm not insurable due to my "pre-existing condition." It's a major setback considering that my big-money days are far behind me and that today my business is simply a labor of love, not of making real money.

Of course, I could have moved back to Canada to avoid all the hospital bills, but the truth is that having to pay the odd $4,000 or even $10,000 hospital bill while traveling the world is still less expensive than living in Canada. It sounds crazy but it's the truth, especially when you are a minimalist and own only two non-running shirts.

2

Of all the surgeries I've had over the years, the one that stands out the most was the surgery that took place in a utility closet. And, I hadn't been sedated.

I was bartending in Edmonton and was scheduled to work the following day which was New Year's Eve. The doctors had told me it would be impossible to work for at least a few days, but most-likely I'd need a full week to recover. I never miss work, so I begged them to help me out. I was told that considering they had to put me under for the surgery, and considering the location and size of my abscess, it just wasn't possible. When I pressed my doctor, he jokingly said that the only way I could leave the hospital the same day was if I wasn't sedated for the procedure. I jumped at the suggestion and my doctor recoiled, thinking I was crazy. He assured me that he had been joking but he admitted it was possible, although he had never done it before.

When I told him that I was game, he set me up in an over-sized closet full of medical devices while more and more doctors and nurses crowded into the room to see the idiot who wanted to be cut open, in a very sensitive place, without being sedated.

My doctor had told me that he would freeze the area but also said that I was going to feel almost everything since the freezing wouldn't be near close enough to where he needed to cut. The abscess was just too large.

I figured that having so many people staring at my bare buttocks and everything else would most likely be more uncomfortable than when I felt him cutting me open. I was wrong.

My girlfriend at the time was permitted in there as well (since half of the hospital staff seemed to be permitted in) and the doctor told her to hold my hand while he cut me open. Before he started, he placed two tongue depressors in my mouth to bite down on.

The instant he started I could feel the

scalpel cutting me open and it was excruciating.

I heard the surgeon ask my girlfriend if I was crying but I let it slide. Then he asked again a few seconds later. When he asked the third time if I was crying, I snapped at him and reminded him that I wasn't unconscious and that no, I wasn't crying but to please hurry up and finish what he was doing. I wasn't sure how much more of it I could endure.

He finally finished what he was doing and I received a round of applause from the crowd of medical professionals that had squeezed into that closet. I was extremely relieved, but I still had to go through the packing procedure.

When they were done, they allowed me to leave the hospital. I could barely walk due to both the pain and the location of the wound. Every step I took pulled on the incision and it was excruciating.

By the following day I only felt marginally better. The area was raw and extremely tender, but I still had to return to the hospital to have the packing removed from the cavity, then refilled. I was offered pain killers but had to turn them down. It was New Year's Eve and I needed to go from the hospital straight to work; I had a bar to tend on the busiest night of the year.

3
Back in Costa Rica after my tumor scare, my health continued to deteriorate and my abscesses became more frequent and harder to deal with. Rather than old abscess points that we learned to deal with on our own, my body started producing more fistulas leading from my intestines to different exit points and in places that required a surgeon's intervention.

I recall one evening in Costa Rica, wondering whether I should fly back to Canada again while yet another abscess was growing. It was just small at the time, but it was growing quickly. Had I not been in so much pain while seated, I would have flown back the next day. Instead, I ended up having surgery that same day instead, costing me just over $10,000.

Less than a week after clearing that bill, I made an appointment with my specialist and booked two tickets back to Canada, again.

4
Upon our return to Canada I met with my specialist who had told me about a new procedure that involved cutting out a crab-apple-sized hunk of flesh from just behind my

testicles. This would remove all the fistulas, or pathways, that had formed between my intestines and nether region. The procedure also involved inserting a Seton ring – a plastic twist tie of sorts that would be inserted into the incision, follow a fistula connected to my colon, then exit via my anus and tie off to the lead end. If it wasn't so horrific to look at, it may have started a new body piercing trend.

As these fistulas were the source of my abscesses, and this procedure meant to end one of the worst side-effects of Crohn's disease for me, I eagerly signed up for it. What I didn't realize at the time was that it would take more than 18 months for me to fully recover.

5

The first phase of recovery was brutal and kept me mostly off my feet for the first few weeks. I then spent another 10 weeks hobbling around with extreme fatigue while trying to figure out how to go about normal daily functions with that Seton ring in the most inconvenient of locations.

I spent a total of three months recovering at my mother's house in Alberta before it was time to head to New York for the marathon. I had abandoned all hope of running the marathon as I hadn't run in months. In fact, since the surgery, I had been wearing diapers to catch the constant discharge and blood from the fistula and incision.

I was slightly depressed from the long and arduous recovery, from being unable to run and from wearing the diapers, of course. I really wanted to run the New York City Marathon for what would have been the seventh time, but it clearly wasn't in the cards.

My girlfriend hadn't seen my situation the same way and had asked me whether I would wear the diaper while running. I recall laughing, wondering why she would assume I was still running as if she hadn't been the one to bathe me and change the packing multiple times a day.

I explained that running was completely out of the question as even walking aggravated the surgery site and Seton.

When she asked me exactly how much it aggravated me to walk with it, I wanted to quickly shoot down what I knew she was thinking. Before I could, however, she went on, reminding me how much I wanted to do the marathon again and that although I wouldn't be able to run the marathon, I could possibly walk it.

Walk a marathon? I thought. Why would I want to do that? It would take me double the time and the diaper, which I clearly needed, would very possibly need changing part way. That didn't seem like an ideal marathon at all.

I shook my head and said no, but thanks.

But it was too late. She had put that little seed of a thought into my head and it started to sprout almost instantly. I thought back to the days I spent hobbling around the school track for charity and how crazy that had seemed at first. Yet I'd done it and I'd done it well. I also inspired myself by not allowing circumstances to control my life or prevent me from doing what I loved most. It was a powerful feeling, one that had eluded me for a few years due to the chronic abscesses, the fatigue and everything else that came with Crohn's. I knew that walking the marathon could help me get back on track.

But...

But I was extremely weak and was honestly worried about being out there on my own under the circumstances, bleeding and dealing with my situation.

I was about to tell her again that it was a crazy idea when she offered to walk it with me.

It floored me. I knew how much she hated to run and exercise in general, so even the mere suggestion made me realize that I had to seriously consider doing it. She had been taking care of me for about four years in ways that most people wouldn't understand unless they'd gone through the same circumstances. I felt a world of gratitude. And here she was, offering to walk 42.2 kilometers with me when I knew she hated to walk two blocks.

As it turned out, I had exactly one spare entry into the marathon. It seemed to be fate.

I put her name on the entry and a few short weeks later, we headed off to the Big Apple.

6

Without a doubt, walking the marathon was one of the most difficult yet rewarding experiences of my life. I had run the New York City Marathon six times previously. Some years I had trained; other years I hadn't run at all in many months leading up to the race. However, those previous marathons all paled in comparison.

I managed to graduate from adult diapers to lining my shorts with maxi pads which made the marathon a little easier than anticipated. A little.

We finished the marathon together after a little less than seven hours, and I had never felt more grateful for her suggestion to walk it. I had also never felt prouder of her. What she did for me melted my heart.

The marathon was extremely painful as every step I took (roughly 55,000 of them) pulled on my incision and eventually it tore open. Sweat ran over that area the entire time, burning and adding to the torture, but when we finished the marathon, I couldn't have been happier.

When we made it back to the hotel, I removed the maxi pads and realized that I would need to go back to diapers for a while. I had bled so much that after the 20-kilometer mark or so, blood had started running down the inside of my right leg. I should have been embarrassed but at the time I had been in too much pain to worry about it.

In total, it took close to a year and a half before my body finally closed up that gaping hole completely and I no longer had to wear the maxi pads or diapers. Perhaps, had we not walked the marathon, I would have healed a few months sooner. However, having that heavy medal placed over my head at the finish line made it more than worthwhile.

7

After New York we returned to Costa Rica for a while, then spent a few months in Europe before flying back to Canada for the summer and the Edmonton Marathon.

I was finally able to start running again. Though it was slow at first, I was just grateful to be at it. I was looking forward to running in Edmonton with some old friends and joining up with a Running Room group. However, as fate would have it, I would once again be sidelined, this time when I tore open my good leg from ankle to knee.

8

As I wasn't marathon ready, nor even half marathon ready, I decided that rather than run any distance at the Edmonton Marathon, I would rent a booth at the race expo for my company and try to sell some tour packages.

I was standing on a heavy-duty collapsing chair while trying to hang my company's banner at the back of my booth when the chair decided to collapse. My left leg, previously known as my good-looking leg, slid through the space between the back and the seat cushion of the chair and I tumbled down.

I remember hitting the floor, embarrassed because I had done so in front of a few people. I was sprawled on the ground, tangled in the chair and ready to hop back up like nothing had happened when Terri, a staff member of mine, started screaming.

I didn't understand why she was reacting the way she was, so I tried to explain that I was fine, just a little sore in the tush and that she was overreacting. She didn't agree and pointed at my leg.

I looked at my right leg, thinking that maybe I twisted it. I looked back at her and said it was fine. However, the look on her face indicated that I wasn't fine – far from it, in fact. She pointed again and I followed her finger. To my horror, I was staring at the inside of my left leg while a 12-inch flap of skin and fat was bunched up and off to one side like a pulled-back curtain.

It was quite horrific to look at and very strange to be looking at the inside of my own leg, but all I could think about was my running. I couldn't tell from looking at my leg how much damage I had done and whether I had just killed any chance of ever running again. I'm fine with blood and the like, having spent so much time in hospitals over the years, so I looked as closely as I could, trying to understand what I had done while waiting for the ambulance to show up.

I could see the muscle. Luckily it looked intact so I held out hope that it would sideline me for only three or four months.

While waiting for the ambulance to show up, I took some extremely graphic photos to send to my mother and keep as a reminder to not stand on folding chairs.

9

I was rushed to the hospital and then made to wait seven hours despite the fact that I had arrived by ambulance. When I was finally attended to, the surgeon who stitched me up told me that I had the skin of an 80-year-old, surely thanks to years of taking daily medication for Crohn's. When my leg had slid through the space at the back of the chair, the fabric on the seat of the chair had literally burnt my leg open, much like one can get a rug burn from a carpet. Of course, what happened to me was a little more severe. Had I been wearing jeans instead of shorts, odds are I wouldn't have flayed my leg open. He also told me that anyone else my age would most likely have simply burnt the hair off their leg, nothing else.

However, I was extremely fortunate that it was the front of my leg that I had injured. Even though I was opened down to the muscle, the surgeon was able to stitch and staple me back up. Today, the evidence is pretty obvious and my previous, good-looking leg now makes my right, twisted leg look much better.

To be honest, though, I couldn't care less about how my leg looks. I spent far too much time worrying about what my right leg looked like to waste another minute worrying about yet another scar on this roadmap of a body. Instead, I wear it with pride, knowing that it's just one more thing that didn't prevent me from accomplishing my goals.

10

Months later, when I was able to run again, I decided that I wanted to participate in the New York City Marathon yet again, but this time by running it.

Unfortunately, yet again, fate still wasn't on my side.

11

The idea behind the major surgery that had included the insertion of the Seton was to prevent future fistulas. Unfortunately, it works only by preventing a fistula from returning to the same place, and, my overachieving intestines produced a network of fistulas that spread out in all directions.

Within three months of my leg mishap, I had another major abscess, then another.

Fortunately, not every abscess led to surgery. Over the years, my ex-wife or my girlfriend would help by cutting me open a little or by poking holes into the abscess with a needle, then draining it. I don't recommend this, but when you're on the plains of the Serengeti, in a remote village in Vietnam or on the Inca Trail in Peru, you do what you have to do. When I wasn't fortunate enough to have someone brave enough to help me, I was forced to get creative with mirrors, cutting myself open, then finding the courage to sit on a hard surface and rock backwards until it took care of itself.

It's not the greatest thing to deal with but I also know that things could be much worse. I only have to think back to the tumor to be grateful for abscesses that I can take care of on my own and that aren't life-threatening.

Plus, each time I started losing energy, I knew that an abscess was coming on. Therefore, I learned to make some quick adjustments to lessen their impact. Of course, my training would stop abruptly. Even if I was running only five or 10 kilometers a day, when the abscesses came on, I felt like I had been training for an ultra-marathon. My body required more sleep, I ate less, and I generally felt terrible. And even though I felt better immediately after surgery, or my DIY home-lancing job, my body still required time to properly recuperate. That being the case and considering that I was averaging between six and eight abscesses a year, running quickly became something that was almost impossible.

Almost.

The truth is, I could have continued training as little as a week or two after each drainage, assuming it was an "at home" drainage. However, my runs would have been greatly reduced. And honestly, it bothered me to go from a comfortable 30-kilometer run to barely making it through three kilometers while wearing a diaper or pads. It wasn't about arrogance or ego; it was simply that I had to work so much harder to get to where I was, only to lose ground time and again. Simply put, it was frustrating.

It was like trying to climb a slippery slope: four steps up, eight steps back. No matter how clean I ate, how hard I trained, it was all wiped away (and more) after every handful of weeks – or so it felt. After a while, I simply gave up and gave in to my disease, assuming this was my destiny. I stopped training.

12

I never told anyone the real reason I wasn't

training, only that I had health issues and only when pressed. Otherwise, I kept everything to myself. I thought my running days were behind me. I just couldn't see the other end of the dark tunnel in which I felt trapped.

Before completely giving up I had spoken with my specialist about refining my diet even further, being more diligent with sleep, controlling stress and basically handling all the known triggers of Crohn's. He simply told me that regardless of what I did, my situation would only continue, worsen or go into remission, then relapse in the future. It wasn't the news I wanted to hear so I gave up on trying so hard and finally accepted that my running days were over.

13

Although it was a hard decision, it seemed like the only one at the time. However, after a few months of assuming that my running days were behind me, my stubbornness returned.

Having my doctors tell me what I could and couldn't do never sat well with me. I asked myself why I would fall into that trap again. I knew my body better than my doctor did and I would do everything I could to get healthy. I didn't care what his other patients had gone through or what the statistics said. I was concerned only with proving him wrong, showing what was possible and what the unexpected looked like. And that's exactly what I did.

14

Despite my constant abscesses, extreme inflammation and stomach pain, and even after going partially blind yet again, this time from pseudo tumors that had formed behind my eyes for about a month (also from Crohn's), my doctor calls me the 'healthiest, sickest patient' he has ever had. It's a title I'm proud to hold, but that's only because I focus on the first part. I honestly don't consider myself sick; I just have to deal with some issues from time to time. We all do.

In my travels, I constantly meet people who make my problems seem ridiculously trivial and who remind me of just how fortunate I truly am. Recently, in India, I saw two different men with two uncorrected Clubfeet. One had been dragging himself along the ground, begging for money, while the other had pulled himself along using a makeshift skateboard. Both had twisted, uncorrected stovepipe legs with severely twisted and under-developed feet. I quickly realized that the only difference between them and me was that I had been lucky enough to be born in Canada. Luck of the draw, nothing else. It has made me realize, time and again, that my problems are only as bad as I allow them to make me feel. We all have obstacles in life. What sets us apart is simply how hard we're willing to fight to overcome those obstacles.

I had spent too much time thinking about all the reasons why I couldn't run rather than thinking about just one reason I had to run.

Sure, I'd been sidelined many times, but I was never out of the game; I'd only acted that way.

Once more, this time as an educated adult, I let my excuses get the better of me. They trampled all over the progress I'd made in my training, my self esteem and my personal power. And it was all my fault.

15

It's one thing to realize the error of your ways, but it's another thing to live with regret and no corrective action. If I had continued feeling sorry for myself I would never have rebounded. I have no doubt my health would have worsened, not gotten better.

Since discovering the tumor and dealing with the last four surgeries, I've never eaten better or exercised more. Every health setback reminded me to stay on track or improve my habits. Of course, my running still needs to catch up to where I was, but now, when I go out for a long run, I don't bleed or feel like I've been run over by a truck. Now I feel that each run is making me stronger, not weaker.

I still have the odd day when the inflammation or pain brings me down and I sulk. However, now those days are few and far between. After dealing with everything that I have, including being on the brink of homelessness, I can clearly see that things always have a way of working out. Always.

Besides, we'll always experience difficulties, from minor ones to extreme ones. If we keep our heads up, we'll always make it to the other side. If life was always fantastic, how would we know to appreciate it? We need the hard times, those days when things go sideways, to truly appreciate when things go well.

16

Today I write from Hue, Vietnam. Tomorrow, I'm scheduled for a 17-kilometer training run at 4AM. It's part of my build-up to the 2018 New York City Marathon. Even though just a month ago I was dreading a five-kilometer run because of yet another abscess, I'm eagerly anticipating tomorrow's run.

It's going to be like that, up and down, and I'm OK with that. Life is always going to be full of ups and downs. What matters is what we do with them. We must try to lessen the impact of the downs, to give them less attention and meaning, while focusing on making the most of the ups.

I've noticed that the more I follow that advice, the healthier I feel. Thinking like that lessens the stress. It allows me to focus on the good and be more accepting of the bad. It has taken the weight off my shoulders and, hence, made me a much happier person. It has allowed me to focus on making my life all it can truly be.

Chapter 15 – It's All About the Mindset

I realized some time ago that, just as my doctor had told me, even if I ate perfectly and got exercise and enough sleep, my health would always keep me on a constant rollercoaster ride. However, I also thought that constantly thinking about it – or worse, worrying about it – wouldn't serve me at all. In fact, it could make matters worse. With that in mind, I decided to stop thinking about it altogether and instead, to focus on how healthy I was, the fact that I had avoided "necessary" intestine-reduction surgery for over 20 years, the fact that I no longer experienced pain after eating or experienced diarrhea or constipation (a big deal for someone with Crohn's) and was able to basically eat freely. And all this despite the fact that I constantly traveled the world and ate foreign food.

This new mindset did more than release stress. It actually helped improve my health and allowed me to focus on living. As my health improved, it also allowed me to stop taking all of the meds that I was on for over two decades.

2

I was always aware of the side effects of daily

medication, like sun sensitivity and thinning skin, which had ultimately led to my severe leg injury. Plus, it was terrible to travel with a year's supply of prescriptions, always having to explain to customs in foreign countries why I was carrying in excess of 4,000 pills, especially when I never had any checked luggage. Apparently, that looks extremely suspect. I've been "randomly" selected for secondary inspection more times than I can count.

After my tumor scare and my decision that it was finally time to change my eating habits, I also decided to start feeding my mind the same way: nothing but proper nutrients in the form of positivity and accepting that which I could not control. When I started noticing how much better I felt, I decided to stop taking one of my medications as a test.

My doctor had figured that they weren't doing as much as they could have been doing for me and suggested that I slowly cut back to half to see how I did. I, of course, took that to mean quit taking the pills altogether and as quickly as possible.

I had previously tried to quit taking my meds when I was still living in Edmonton, but I'd always ended up in the hospital for my efforts. However, during those previous attempts, I had also been drinking more than I should have and was eating very poorly. I figured that this time, if I continued to watch what went into my mouth, perhaps I would fare better.

Within three months of deciding to start cutting back I was medication-free for the first time in over 21 years. It was a fantastic feeling to be free of so many harmful chemicals. I started feeling even better yet within just a week of being medication-free; within a few weeks I had started feeling better than I could ever remember. I still formed abscesses at the same rate as when I took the meds, but in general I felt more energetic and healthier. In fact, if it weren't for the abscesses and inflammation, I wouldn't have any symptoms at all.

Today, six years later, I'm still completely medication-free.

3

Shortly after ending my marriage and my 10-year career, I honestly thought that I had improved my health. However, the really big improvements didn't come until I accepted my disease and stopped taking the meds. Once I realized this on some subconscious level, I realized that I hadn't been ready to get better back then.

If we're really honest with ourselves, there's always a payoff or benefit to staying sick, overweight, poor, single, etc. The most obvious payoff is that these things provide wonderful excuses for why we're stuck in life. For instance, if someone is afraid of being hurt in a relationship, it's easier to stay single and come up with excuses for why they are single rather than admitting the fear, taking the chance on a relationship and accepting that it may or may not work out.

I think I continued to abuse food and blame Crohn's because I was afraid of being truly healthy. Truly healthy means learning more about nutrition, working hard on my body, giving up on certain favorite foods, limiting others and a general lifestyle change. It also means loving oneself fully and accepting that failure is possible, both of which can be brutally difficult at times. And, it's also a lot of commitment. It's much easier to simply think that none of that is possible due to 'my situation', thus releasing oneself from the burden of becoming a healthier person.

It sounds ridiculous, but it's also extremely common. It's like thinking, 'I'll go for my run tomorrow because today I'm not feeling tip-top. I just want to sit on the sofa and watch a movie and eat a bag of chips.' It's so much easier to do that then make a real change. And some of us are really good at it because it's the norm and we're used to failing, not winning.

Before truly healing myself, this was my mindset some days, just another way of giving up my personal power and falling victim to my demons – something I've done more than a few times and despite knowing better.

Having grown up with an appreciation of how short life truly is, due to my father's passing when he was just 31, I had decided at a young age that I would live my life to the fullest. I had no desire to live with regrets or 'should haves' or 'could haves' as we never know when our time will be up. Yet, looking back, I can see that although I've done a fairly good job of following that overall, there was a lot of room for improvement.

I also realized that another big part of real healing is accepting the past, including past mistakes. Rather than beat myself up about something I can't change, I only have to look forward and focus on what I can change: my future.

Today, I try to live with intention. I try to better myself as a person, a runner, a partner and a business owner. I spend my time constantly refining my life and looking to enrich it. Where previously I traveled almost aimlessly, over-indulging and hitting as many countries as possible without any other real goals, today I fill my days with all the things most important to me. They are the things that make me jump out of bed early every morning and be truly grateful for every new day. At least five days a week, I do every single thing on my "if today were my last day on earth, I would do" list. It's pretty amazing to spend each day like that – a lot like finding heaven on earth.

Of course, getting to this point took a lot of risks but none of them scared me more than the idea of not risking what I had for a better way of life – a way of life that made me truly happy. Yet I can't tell you how many people I've met, rich or poor, from all walks of life and countries around the world, who call me 'lucky.' It's a word I don't care for because nothing fell into my lap by accident or by 'luck.' I worked hard to achieve the life of my dreams, and I'm proud of that work.

Usually, if I chat more extensively with one of those people, they will eventually tell me that they wished they could do something similar with their own life – make a major change and do something that they've always put off or realize a dream they let slip away. It's sad when I hear this. I try to explain that they still can, but it almost always falls on deaf ears. People tend to stick to what they know, what's easier or what's safe, for better or worse.

Whenever I meet these people, I use it as a reminder of where I was myself, then take another close look at my life to make sure I'm truly living the life I want and not allowing my fears to get in the way.

4

I feel that during the past six years I've been virtually spot on while I continue focusing on traveling and running, my health and all the little things that make me truly happy.

In those short six years I've had many ups and downs, but the ups have far outweighed the downs. Meanwhile, the downs have turned out to be blessings in disguise, or at least valuable lessons.

During those half-dozen years, I lost another $125,000, which was every dime I had ever saved (and a little more) since I'd almost gone bankrupt and left Canada. I bounced back from that as well and have made it to my 18th year of business, surpassing even my own expectations.

I can't say that the past 18 years of running my business have been easy, but I would never call it difficult. It's allowed me to live the life of my dreams – a life that couldn't possibly make me any happier and that I wouldn't change for anything.

MOSHI, TANZANIA 2008

I'm standing in Moshi Stadium, a short drive from Mt. Kilimanjaro in Tanzania, East Africa. It's completely dark and only a few runners have shown up so far, but I want to get to the starting area a little early to take some photos while the sun rises, illuminating the highest peak in Africa.

Today I'll be running the Kilimanjaro Marathon with some of the world's fastest marathon runners and more than a few Olympians. I'm hoping that in attendance will be one of my personal heroes: former Olympian John Stephen Akhwari, whom Time Magazine had dubbed "the world's greatest last place finisher" because he hadn't given up after taking a terrible spill at the 1968 Olympics in Mexico City.

This will be one of four times I've returned to this stadium but today will be my first time running the marathon. I've wanted to run the marathon since I first started offering tour packages here, but my health had never cooperated. Though I was sick each time in the past, I did always manage to run one of the shorter distances offered, including the half marathon. Today, however, I feel great and my training has gone very well.

2

More people are filing into the stadium and I can see that I'm clearly outclassed. However, no one – myself included – seems to care. I'm grateful to be running on the turf of some of the world's fastest runners as well as some of the kindest and most interesting runners.

The sun still hasn't fully come up and we're already lining up to start. A group of teenagers that I met the previous day has come up to say hello. I've sponsored each of them to run today and their gratefulness makes me feel a little stronger.

We start running out of the stadium and through the neighboring villages to the cheers of a few locals. Young children, somewhere between the ages of five and seven, decide to join by running alongside the handful of foreigners. It's a sight to see as some are wearing flip-flops at best. Most, however, are barefoot.

3

The Kilimanjaro Marathon has a punishing route that includes a 10-kilometer hill. However, as the sun starts to rise and as Mt. Kilimanjaro becomes more visible, the views make the course more bearable. It's a dream to be running here and I can't help but smile.

To my right, two young boys, one about six and the other no older than eight, see me smiling and take it as a sign to run over and join me. They flank me on either side, grabbing my hands and telling me "Haraka, haraka," which means, in a very direct way, to pick up the pace.

I do, but it's short-lived as the hill is punishing and I've only just begun it.

I assume that the boys will leave me after a few hundred meters or maybe, at most, one kilometer. I can't see how they could run more considering one is in sandals and the other is barefoot. However, an hour later, they're still at my side, gripping my sweaty hands fiercely.

4

We come to a water station and they refuse to take any water while I feel like I'm drinking enough for four grown men. I basically force it on them and they finally take it, then pour the cups over their heads. We share a laugh and I see them eyeing the cola. I grab them each a cup which they happily drink. Then we're on our way again, both of them tightly gripping my hands on either side once more.

I wonder what their parents think, realizing we're at least 10 kilometers from where they'd started running with me. I think that maybe they'll turn around and start running home, but they don't. Instead, they continue climbing that hill with me to the very top.

5

The sun is beating down on us now and I can't imagine how these young children are not only keeping up but wanting me to run faster. The road must be incredibly hot for the child without shoes, yet he isn't complaining. I realize why it's countries like Tanzania that produce some of the world's greatest runners. I'm beyond impressed. I'm also extremely tired while these two kids haven't even broken a sweat.

We share some laughs when they try to communicate with me and I have no idea what they're saying. I'm sure it's along the lines that I'm running too slow, so I decide to tell them some stories in English, just to pass the time. They seem to listen along, gripping my hands even tighter. I know they don't understand anything but are seemingly happy to be running with me. I, on the other hand, am more than happy and grateful for these two kids, making this marathon very special.

6

We make it up the hill, turn around and

immediately start back down it. We run back through the same villages, this time to the cheers of a few more people.

Each water station is a repeat performance of the kids dumping the water on their heads and chugging the cola, then burping and laughing. I decide to join them with a cup of cola at one station. I quickly regret the decision, burping uncontrollably and making them laugh even more.

I want to walk but the boys won't allow it. They pull me along, forcing me to pick up the pace. Soon I realize that I don't need to walk; I just want to. Their mental fortitude, at their young ages, makes me feel especially weak. I make a mental note to learn from them.

7

The course works its way through the farmland and villages at the base of Mt. Kilimanjaro, providing stunning views the majority of the way. I can't help but feel great despite the punishing course. Locals are singing and clapping even though now only foreigners are on the course. All the locals finished long before.

I finally start to recognize where I am, and I realize that we're down to the final kilometer. Still gripping my hands with surprising force, my two friends, Barefoot and Sandals, are still on either side. By my calculation, they've run at least 32 kilometers with me. Even though I know it to be true, I still can't wrap my head around it.

8

As we start running into the stadium for a three-quarter lap before crossing the finish line, I feel the boys start to let go of my hands. In the past three-and-a-half hours or so, the only other times they let go of my hands was at the water stations. Now, as they start to do it again, I think that maybe they're not allowed to run inside the stadium.

I grip their hands tighter and drag them until they understand, then they continue to run with me.

We get about halfway around the track while everyone is cheering and I'm beaming ear to ear, grateful for another marathon, one I'll never forget, when the boys try to break free once more. I try my best to keep them with me, but they shake themselves free, then wave me on. They know that this is my race and refuse to cross the finish line with me. However, that's the only way I want to end my marathon, with my two little companions at my side. They deserve this finish more than I do, but there's no persuading them. They're already off, running towards the stadium seating.

9

I cross the finish line, grateful to be done but unhappy to do so on my own. After collecting my medal, I immediately go looking for the boys even though I'm told that John Stephen Ahkwari is also in the stadium. I've always wanted to meet him and it's never worked out, but right now the two boys are more important. I need to thank them and maybe find an interpreter.

When I eventually find them, they offer me some fruit and shake my hand, congratulating me. Then they take off running before I can get a picture of them. They leave me there in awe. This was just another day for them yet it's a day I will never forget.

10

Although I'm exhausted, I try to find John Stephen, but I hear that he has left as well. Meeting him will need to wait until the next time I come back to Moshi, Tanzania.

As luck would have it, I did get my chance eight years later, and it was certainly worth the wait.

Some of the kids I sponsored

...and their shoes

I finally meet John Stephen Akhwari

Epilogue

I've spent the past 14 years with no fixed address, traveling the world non-stop and out of just a carry-on bag, while operating Dream Travel and focusing on what makes me the happiest. I made it all happen by being honest about my fears and taking leaps of faith, repeatedly.

When I first was forced to leave Canada to keep the business afloat, I had no idea what would come of my business or my life. However, I trusted myself to do whatever it took. I also knew that I was stronger than my excuses and fears, even if I fell victim to them a few times.

To date, I've run in roughly 80 of the 100 countries and territories I've been to, including marathons on five of them. That doesn't count the countries I'm not allowed to admit I've been to.

I've been blessed to run with and meet some of the world's greatest runners, including some who changed the sport, like Kathrine Switzer, John Stephen Akhwari, Dean Karnazes and Pravin Zele.

I'm nothing short of blessed and will always be grateful for the challenges that were laid out for me at birth. They gave me a reason to push myself, to reach for new heights and to show that the word *impossible* exists only in my fears. Besides, if there's one thing that I've learned in my years of traveling and running, it's that winning isn't just about finishing another race, but getting up every time life knocks me back down. That's the real challenge, but one that I now face with confidence.

That's important as I know that I'll never win a marathon and I'll most likely never beat my fastest time. I know that my best days are behind me. My right leg, ankle and foot seem to give me more trouble than they used to and eventually I'll have to retire my running shoes. I'm OK with all of that. But until I'm forced to stop, I assure you that I'll be out there, somewhere on this big, beautiful blue marble, running.

The 2018 TCS New York City Marathon is now just a little more than a month away and my girlfriend and I have been successfully training while traveling through the Americas, Europe and Asia. Our weekly long runs for this marathon will have taken place in eight countries and on four continents.

Although running distance has started to become painful once more, and my right foot twisting more than it has in years, I'm still giving it my best. Pain is an old friend who reminds me that I'm still alive. I'll get through this training and I'll run the marathon, there's absolutely no doubt in my mind.

Running has not only been my passion and business, but also a cure. When I first started running, my right foot straightened out more – something the surgeries couldn't do for me. When I wasn't able to run for longer periods of time, my foot started to curve again, giving me a gentle reminder that maybe in fact I was born to run after all, or if nothing else, that it's what my body wants and needs. That may be changing now, but I'll continue to fight it for as long as I can.

In my early 20s I thought that I had the perfect excuse to not run, however I learned that this was just another way of me avoiding my fears. Fortunately, I also learned that having fears is acceptable, but that even better than accepting fears is when you crush them under your feet while running well beyond what anyone thinks possible.

Follow Stephen, his travels and running at:

www.dreamtravelcanada.com

www.instagram.com/dreamtravelcanada

www.facebook.com/dreamtravelcanada

Or run with Stephen here:
www.strava.com/athletes/32357722

Made in USA - Kendallville, IN
65227_9781798107522
10.09.2025 0956